The Good, the Mad and the Ugly:
The Andy Morrison Story

The Good, the Mad and the Ugly: The Andy Morrison Story

Andy Morrison
(with David Clayton)

Fort Publishing Ltd

First published in 2011 by Fort Publishing Ltd, Old Belmont House,
12 Robsland Avenue, Ayr, KA7 2RW

Printed by Ozgraf

Front-cover photograph courtesy of Action Images

Graphic design by Mark Blackadder

Typeset by Kerrypress Ltd

ISBN: 978-1-905769-27-8

For my dad, who has always been and always will be my inspiration.

Contents

Acknowledgements		9
Foreword by Joe Royle		11
1	'What the Fuck Have I Done This Time?'	15
2	'I Was Having It, All Day Long'	21
3	A Pilgrim's Dream	33
4	Nightmare on Union Street	47
5	Fish Out of Water	61
6	King Kenny Rules	67
7	Tangerine Dream	79
8	Just One Notch Below Attempted Murder	85
9	Pig Sick	93
10	'Fucking Hell, Mozzer . . . I See You're Still at It'	97
11	Terrier by Name . . .	105
12	The Great Escape, Parts One and Two	111
13	Whacking Jacko	121
14	Captain of City	131
15	Licker Licence	143
16	Loan Ranger	151
17	Last-Chance Saloon	159
18	Pushed to the Brink	169
19	A Slug in the Guts	177
20	Another Demon Put to Bed	185
21	Doing a Cantona	197
22	It's Not Where You're From . . .	213
23	Dream Team	219
Career Statistics		223

Acknowledgements

First of all I would like to thank my wife Paula for her love, support and friendship through the good and bad times and for giving me the most precious things in my life: Azza, Bam Bam and Cha Cha, my three children who are better known as Arron, Brooke and Charley. I love you all so much.

Thanks to my mum Anne and stepfather Barry. Mum, when I see your patience, warmth and love with your grandchildren, it reminds me how fortunate I was to have your love and guidance as a young boy. Yours is a gentle love and it is thanks to you that I am now able to show my children the same. To my brothers Ian and Graham, whom I love dearly, and to my little brother Cathel who we lost too soon; I miss you so much.

To my grandmother Alice Jo, whom I adored, and who showed me that your loyalties should always be to your family. To my grand-dad Charlie: I hope to listen to your passion for Scotland and the Morrison clan for many years to come. To Sybil my dad's partner and my in-laws Beryl and Burt: thanks for always being there for us. To Ron, Paula's father, who we sadly lost many years ago; I still miss your warmth and smile. To John, Nick, Andrew and Sharon, my brothers- and sisters-in-law: thanks for the memories and friendship. To Tom Austin and Freddy Toms – the Clough and Taylor of Devon junior football – what a team we had! To Alec Brenton and Dave Lamey for taking me to Argyle as a fifteen-year-old. To Dave Smith who gave me my first contract and Martin Harvey and Malcolm Musgrove for my early guidance at Argyle when I was as raw as they come. To Dave Kemp for having faith in me and pushing me forward and giving me belief. To big Sam Allardyce and Brian Horton for signing me and making me the proud captain of Blackpool and Huddersfield respectively, I still feel I let you both down. To Joe Royle and Willie Donachie for being so much more than a great manager and coach. To Andy and Andrea Preece for your friendship and love over the years and for Preecey for getting me some great moves, I couldn't have done it without you pal. Sheffield Gordon and all the friends of Bill W who have helped me stay sober – one day at a time, right? To Danny Rokstar for our long chats and utter drivel which keeps us both well. To all the troops from the Barbican; you know who you are! To James McCarroll, my publisher, for having faith in this project. To Dave Clayton and his family for allowing him to write my story over the past year. I'm looking forward to the follow up!

Thanks to all the unbelievable supporters I've been lucky enough to play in front of at Argyle, Blackpool, Huddersfield and particularly Manchester City; I was never prouder than when skippering the Blues at Wembley.

Finally, I've left this bit until last on purpose because without my father, I wouldn't be telling my story at all. Dad, you have been my inspiration and guidance for as long as I can remember and you continue to inspire me to go on and achieve my dreams.

Andy Morrison
Cheshire
June 2011

Foreword

By
Joe Royle

I first saw Andy Morrison as a raw youngster playing for Plymouth Argyle in 1991. He was in midfield back then and I liked his style and commitment immediately. He always played on an edge and you knew there was an unusual mix of a physical presence matched with a great touch. The ball was his friend and was never a problem for him, but, though he seemed a great prospect, he seemed to lose his way in the years after.

He went to Blackburn and didn't play much, but he was a squad member when they won the Premier League and the fact Kenny Dalglish signed him speaks volumes for his ability.

By his mid-twenties, there were rumours circulating that he was having one or two off-field problems. It was well known he had one or two anger-management issues and that he also liked a drink and he seemed to drift around for a while from club to club, but I knew he was better than that.

I was manager at City and we were struggling to come to terms with the third tier of English football during the 1998/99 season. What we needed more than anything was a leader and sometimes in football you need a lucky break and that's what we got. Les Chapman, our kit manager, lived on the Huddersfield side of Oldham and he'd been at Huddersfield Town previously, so had good connections with the club.

He came in one day and said, 'Big Andy's had a bust-up with Peter Jackson.'

It was fairly well-known that Andy's knees weren't the best, but he was within our market, I knew the player fairly well and he was a leader, something Willie Donachie and I had identified as the main thing lacking in our squad. The scenario was perfect because Huddersfield manager Peter Jackson wanted Andy out, Andy wanted to leave and we quickly agreed an initial loan fee of £35,000, taking into consideration that his knee would never pass a medical.

We had a youngish side and they had been under the cosh for the best part of three years during which time they had been relegated twice. They were nowhere near ready or up to the task of living up to the hopes and expectation of the Maine Road crowd. We needed a larger-than-life figure to grab them by the scruff of their necks, instil belief and help turn things around; Andy ticked all the boxes.

When he signed we heard all the usual comments about signing a journeyman and a player at the wrong end of his career, but on his debut against Colchester, his first tackle saw him launch one of their lads with a perfectly fair, but thunderous tackle – the sort we hadn't seen in a long time. Then he goes and scores the winning goal in the last minute, following that up with a superb volleyed goal at Oldham that Jermain Defoe would have been proud of. In just two games we'd taken six points and we'd seen two sides of Andy as a player – the uncompromising defender and the technically astute footballer.

There is no doubt he was the catalyst that turned our season around.

I've been in management a long time and without question Andy is one of the best signings I ever made and as I've gone on record as saying before, he dragged us kicking and screaming out of division two in that first season. He found a club that suited him down to the ground and I think it's fair to say the supporters found a warrior on the pitch to channel their passion.

He's also a great lad, a fantastic professional who only missed training once, but came in the next day to apologise, where he explained what had happened. He had gone up to Inverness to see his family and, well, it all got a bit messy, shall we say.

I said, 'Andy, you're going to need help.'

He told me he knew exactly what he needed to do and from that day to this, he has never touched a drop of alcohol. That takes some doing and he did it because he wanted to change his life for the better – something he should be very proud of. Had he reformed sooner, I've no doubt he would have been a Premier League player for many years and would have won many caps for Scotland.

His ability was more deserving of the top division: he knew the game, was excellent on the ball, was outstanding in the air and for someone who isn't the tallest centre back in the world, he would compete with anyone and more often than not win the challenge. If you beat Andy Morrison in the air, you were doing well. He was as tough as they come, but a great lad with it. He was no trouble to me whatsoever and was my right arm on the pitch.

We had a few lads at the club back then who enjoyed a drink so he was coming into an environment that could have been tempting for him to go the other way, but he didn't. He led Manchester City with great pride and, without going over the top, his contribution to the club was a pivotal point in its history and its future.

In the following pages, there will be moments and events that will shock you, but by the time you've finished the book, you'll also understand better the reasons he did some of the things he did during his life. Take it from me; he's an honest, decent lad who made a few bad decisions, but then, who hasn't? For the effort he made to get his life back on track, he has my admiration.

There was Shaun Goater with his goals, Nick Weaver with his saves and Andy Morrison with his leadership. He's up there with the best and trust me, one of the most important players Manchester City have ever had.

I saw him recently on a golf course in Cheshire and he's a beautiful boy, pleasant and lovely to talk to I'm forever in his debt for what he did for me and my team when I was manager at City. I can only wish him well for the future, thank him again and I look forward to watching his progress in coaching because people like Andy don't come along very often in football and he has got a lot to offer the game.

Joe Royle, March 2011

1

'What the Fuck Have I Done This Time?'

It is six o'clock on a Friday morning. I wake up not knowing where I am or why I'm there. I see four, whitewashed brick walls and I get a sinking feeling in the pit of my stomach.

Oh, fuck. Not again . . .

I felt sick, disgusted with myself. What had I done this time, and, more to the point, how much trouble was I in? Maybe this would be the one that would finish my career and something inside me half-wished it would because I'd been on self-destruct for too long. It needed to end, one way or another.

I had never done things by half so I knew that whatever had led me to this police cell would be a result of violence in one form or another. I feel my face. It's sore and my eye is swollen. My knuckles are scraped and painful. Fuck.

I couldn't believe I had allowed this to happen, especially with things going so well for me. I had just needed that release, another long session that would stop me thinking how fucking pointless I was. I sat up, turned around and smashed my forehead into the wall with as much energy as I had left in me. I felt nothing but hatred for myself, but that was nothing new. I had spent my whole life with a loaded gun aimed at my head with my own fingers on the trigger. I kept spinning the chamber, waiting for the time it finally landed on the bullet. Had this been it? In my mind, the normal part was punishing the other Andy Morrison, the one that appeared when I drank myself to oblivion, but it was getting harder and harder to differentiate between the two. I couldn't see there was no dividing line at that point.

The gash on my head had smeared bright red blood onto that whitewashed cell wall and I wiped it across the surface and considered doing it again and again until I had punished myself enough. I felt no pain, just rage at my stupidity and weakness. Like I said, I was fucking useless. I had to bring the cycle to an end because what I was living wasn't a life. I was in a place so dark I couldn't see any light and I realised that, wherever the brink was, I had reached it.

What the fuck had I done? Had I killed someone? Put someone in the hospital? Or was it a minor misdemeanour that just warranted a cooling-off period in a cell? It was the not knowing that was killing me. Imagine being sat there, your future hanging in the balance, waiting to tip one way or the other. I needed to know so I could take whatever was coming my way and get on with it.

I didn't have to wait too long to find out. The grill on my cell door slid back and a police officer peered through, accusingly.

'Oh, awake are we?'

'Yeah,' I sighed, feeling the gash on my head. The blood had stopped.

The desk sergeant opened the door and invited me to follow him down the corridor. As we walked, he sniffed and then asked, 'Where's Rambo from last night, then?'

Why the fuck had he said that? What did it mean? I will never forget those words or the way he said them. I had nothing left in me. The comparison could only mean I was up to my neck in shit. He led me to the custody sergeant who took my fingerprints, a DNA swab and then began to read a sheet of charges. I could see through the white paper that it filled the best part of a page.

Apparently I'd been involved in a fight in an Irish bar in Inverness the night before and had been escorted out of the pub by two doormen after getting a bit loud. As we approached the exit, one of them belted me on the back of the head, pushing me out of the back entrance. I turned and ran back towards the pub, putting my head straight through the glass door they had hurriedly closed. I crashed through the door and grabbed the guy who had hit me, dragging him outside before setting about him in the car park.

I was charged with criminal damage, assault on the doorman, threatening behaviour towards the arresting officers, criminal damage to the police car, assault and threatening behaviour to the custodial sergeant, six charges all told. I just sat there in a daze as they reeled them off. They might just as well have been talking about somebody else because I had no recollection of those events. But then, I never did when I blacked out during a drinking session.

I was released on bail and went straight back to the bar where it had kicked off the night before. I found the manager and asked him if I could pay for damaging his door. He was pretty relaxed about it and told me that kind of thing happened every weekend. I gave him £140 there and then and apologised for the mess I had caused. He told me he had closed-circuit-television footage of the doorman punching me as I was being escorted out and that he'd take that into account. He later sacked the doormen and dropped the charges, as did the doorman, not that it made me feel any better. Still, I was off the hook again.

I jumped in my car and was soon driving up towards Kinlochbervie, which is a hundred miles north of Inverness. It may have been the back end of beyond, but it still felt like home and it was also where my dad lived. I'd only stopped in Inverness to chill out, have a few drinks and then rest overnight before driving on, but, of course, it didn't pan out that way.

I unpacked on arrival, threw my overnight bag in the spare room and spent the entire weekend in an alcohol-fuelled daze. I think, deep down, I was trying to drink until the pain went away for good, or at least get pissed enough to forget that I would have to face my manager when I got back. At one point I woke up in the pub in which I had spent most of the day and sat there, tears rolling down my face but not knowing why I was crying.

'Fucking stop it you soft cunt,' a voice inside my head chided. 'Stop fucking crying, you pussy. Don't show any emotion.'

It was a voice I was familiar with; it came when I was at my lowest ebb. I'd had enough but didn't know what to do. The voice came back again. 'Just fucking end it now, you prick.' I was sick of letting people down and apologising and promising it wouldn't happen again, then doing it all again. If you had given me a polygraph test, I would have passed every time because I meant it and sincerely wanted the carnage to stop each time I said it. However, I never told anyone I'd never drink again.

There were two potential solutions.

One was easy and quick and would sort my problems out once and for all. An uncle had a 2.2 rifle he kept in his garage for shooting rabbits and foxes. I knew exactly where it was and it was just ten minutes away. I could get my hands on it, walk into the field behind his house and instantly put a stop to this mess. The only thing holding me back was the thought of my wife and kids discovering what had happened. Even if I didn't deserve better, they did.

I also knew it was the coward's way out and while I may be many things, a coward isn't one of them. But for Paula and the kids, I think I would have done it; instead of which I carried on drinking throughout the afternoon and evening, trying to blot everything out as per usual.

I hadn't been sober for two days and just before eleven on the Sunday night, as the pub was about to close, I ordered eight cans of lager and a half bottle of vodka. The girl behind the bar, a family friend, asked, 'Are you sure, Andy?'

I thought it through and replied: 'No, you're right; I'd better take twelve cans.'

That was my state of mind. I honestly thought she was concerned about whether I had enough booze to get me through the night. I paid for my carry-out and left before driving to Drummond Pier, a place I knew well from my childhood. It lies two miles outside of the village and is a quiet, lonely place after dark.

It might as well have been the edge of the world.

I parked up and as the wind and rain battered the car I put a CD on and just sat there all night with my cans and my vodka and drank the lot before sunrise. I'd put the booze in the foot-well behind my seat and every time I reached back and could feel a couple of cans clang together, I felt fine, knowing there was more to come. I picked up the last one at six, felt around the floor and was disappointed to discover I had no more left.

I'd spent the best part of four days drinking solidly and yet I still hadn't had enough. I drove back home and went to sleep, waking up around midday feeling sick and physically shit. Something felt different. I felt more desperate and alone than I'd ever done before. This wasn't a life, just a prison sentence with no hope of parole.

I sank to my knees and let out a heartfelt cry. 'Please fucking help me. I can't take any more of this.'

I lay on my bed for a time, a million thoughts spinning round my head. This was the day I always knew would come. I either faced the fact that I was a chronic alcoholic and got help – or went back to the pub. It could have gone either way because I knew another session would blot everything out, at least for a while, but, perhaps for the first time, I pushed that thought out of my mind.

I decided the thing I wanted more than anything was to finally sort my life out. I wasn't a kid anymore and I wasn't washed up wondering where it had all gone wrong: I was an important part of Manchester City Football Club, just in case you were wondering where all this shit fitted into my career. I wasn't ready to give up on my family, the club or myself. I now accepted that I just couldn't drink alcohol anymore, because, once I started, I couldn't stop. In my mind, things had finally fallen into place. It was a pivotal moment.

I had something to eat, drank endless cups of coffee and watched some television. The next day, I drove back to Manchester and headed straight for the training ground at Platt Lane. I arrived about quarter past nine and Roy Bailey the club physio was waiting for me.

'You're in fucking trouble,' he said. I smiled and told him I knew. Joe Royle and Willie Donachie were in the office and I knocked on the door before walking in. Joe looked at me and shook his head.

'What the hell are you doing, Andy?' he asked. 'And more to the point: why? You've hardly put a foot wrong since you came here and made all the right impressions on and off the pitch. Why would you risk throwing all that away with all this insanity? You need help.'

I didn't want to explain myself to Joe. I was tired of explaining my actions, having given the same old excuses to fifteen different managers over the years, swearing that I would never do it again, that I had seen the light, all that bollocks, though of course I meant every word at the time. It was time to stop bullshitting.

'Look, I know what I need to do. This is it. The madness ends here and now. Trust me Joe, I won't let you down. I'm gonna sort this out.'

This time I meant it.

Joe nodded. He knew from the way I said it that I was serious.

Three years before I had been sent a pamphlet by a friend after another of my scrapes. The pamphlet had fifteen questions about your relationship with alcohol. If you answered yes to three out of fifteen, chances were you had a serious problem. I answered yes to thirteen out of fifteen. At that time, I wasn't ready to look at my drinking because I was enjoying it too much, but nonetheless it had planted a seed in my mind, one that was now bearing fruit.

Two days later I attended the first of many Alcoholics Anonymous meetings in Sheffield. My addictive nature ensured I was hooked straight away.

'My name's Andy and I am an alcoholic.'

A weight lifted immediately.

I knew I had a real chance of beating it. I bought into what they were saying and I began a new life away from dependence on alcohol. As I write this now, I have gone without the want or the need for a drink for almost thirteen years. One day at a time.

I can't say there haven't been one or two violent episodes since, though I'll let you judge what you would have done in my shoes. The journey to the point I'm now at, however, makes me think the following pages are about somebody else. It's been an eye-opener, but a cathartic one at that. The path I've trodden has been anything but straight and narrow and there's loads of stuff I'd rather gloss over and pretend never happened. I'm not trying to glorify anything. I just want to tell the truth.

I am going to reveal everything that has happened in my life, good, mad and often ugly, even if it is painful for me to rake over. In fact, fuck it.

Let's tell it exactly like it was.

2

'I Was Having It, All Day Long'

Every story needs a beginning and mine starts north of the border in Kinlochbervie, in the county of Sutherland, at the age of eight. With a population of less than five hundred, Kinlochbervie is a small fishing village where everyone knows everyone else's business and it about as isolated from the rest of Scotland as you could get. KLB, as it is often referred to by locals, is the most northerly port on the west coast of Britain. The nearest supermarket is sixty miles away and the bank and the cinema both arrive on the back of a lorry. Like I said, it felt like a million miles from anywhere.

The winters were bitter, the summers cool and we were exposed to the elements on a daily basis. It was a tough place to live and the people who lived there matched the environment. Generations of Morrisons came from the area – Morrison is by far the most common name – and I felt happy and secure with a fairly settled home life and a great group of friends.

Our home was by a loch and I loved everything about the place. I was a true Highlander and couldn't have been happier. My grandma's house, in nearby Polin Bay, was next to the beach and I would spend whole summers playing there, guarding the beach from the English with my wooden gun. It was magical and I was in love with Scotland and my life.

Then, one day, everything changed. I was in the school playground with my mates, having a laugh and enjoying myself. I loved the school, loved my mates and hadn't a care in the world, or so I thought. At lunchtime my dad arrived at the gates and shouted me over. He was a fisherman and it was unusual to see him at school, especially at that time of day. I wondered what was going on. He told me to get my stuff and jump in the back of the car. My brothers Ian, 11, and Graham, 3, were there and my baby brother Cathel was in his car seat with my mum sat in the front. Dad shut the door, got in, started the engine and drove off. He said nothing. Nobody did. I looked around. The car was packed full of cases and boxes and it was a tight squeeze. I realised this was more than a family day out.

'Where we going, Dad?' I asked.

'Plymouth.'

'Plymouth? On holiday? Why? What about school?'

'Don't worry about that, son. It's a long drive. Get some sleep.'

As we drove up Big Brae, the hill that led into our village, I looked back and could see our home, my school and my mates standing at the railings watching us pull further and further away. It would be three years before I'd see them or my village again, though my heart and spirit would remain in the Highlands.

Dad was right about the long trip. It was 750 miles to be precise and took us fourteen hours. That was the first I knew of what Mum and Dad had been planning. I had not been told there was even the possibility of leaving Scotland, but there it was. My parents had decided they needed a change, though I would later learn there was a bit more to it than simply a change of scenery.

Plymouth was at the other end of the British Isles and was about as far from Kinlochbervie and my old life as you could get. I wasn't unfamiliar with the city, though, because my mum had been born and raised in Plymouth and my dad had served there during his time in the Royal Marines. It was an obvious place to settle as far as they were concerned, but my head was spinning. I was devastated. I was leaving my entire world behind, but I suppose when you're a kid aged eight, you don't get much say in these matters, do you?

We were exhausted at the end of the journey, but we had a place all ready to move into and our new home would be number 5 St Anne's Road, Glenholt. Within a few days we started at new schools. Ian and I were the new kids and obviously had broad Scottish accents, which made us stand out even more, but we had to make new friends and try to fit in.

We were both nicknamed Jock from day one, a name that would stick throughout our lives. Ian didn't waste any time establishing a pecking order at our new school. He was in the most senior year and within two days he had found the top boy and informed him that he would be taking over. The other lad didn't challenge him and that was it – it was just something he had to do. Why? I'm not sure, but for Langley junior school, it was like the second coming of the Krays.

For the first three or four weeks, I dreamt of my old life and the friends I'd left behind. I missed my house and Loch Innes opposite, my old school and going to Gran's house and I missed Scotland so much. Maybe if I had known the move was on the cards I would have handled it better but it had been a massive upheaval. It broke my heart if truth be told.

There was worse to come, too. I don't think we had been in Plymouth for three months when my parents decided to split up. Dad always worked hard and played hard but the marriage was obviously in trouble because there was invariably a bad atmosphere in the family home, not to mention many heated arguments. Mum and Dad hadn't been getting on and it must have been the last throw of the dice to move away from KLB and try to start afresh. However, whatever issues my parents had they took them all the way to Plymouth; if anything, they got worse. Perhaps because she now had a support network around her in the place she had been raised, Mum felt confident enough to branch out on her own.

Ian, Graham and I were close to Dad and the thought of him not being around profoundly affected us, but he moved into a flat nearby and we still got to see him fairly regularly. In time we accepted what had happened and gradually immersed ourselves in our new life in Plymouth. We saw Dad at weekends and the first time he dropped us back home, we stood at the gate watching as he drove away. He looked back, waved and I saw him wipe away a tear. I have never forgotten that moment because he wasn't one for showing emotion and I had certainly never seen him cry before.

Ian was only eleven, but he was a headstrong character who didn't really fit into the education system and he became more and more difficult for Mum to cope with. Out of options, she had no choice out to send Ian to a strict boarding school in Torquay. When he was home, we would fight all the time. I could box and had a lot of natural ability, but Ian couldn't, so we would go out into the garden and wrap socks or bandages around our hands. To get things started, I'd take the piss out of him, feint to the left, then clip his ear and taunt him until he took the bait. He would grab me and rub my face in the grass, laughing as he did it. Dad didn't seem to mind. In fact he enjoyed our little sparring sessions, so long as they didn't get out of hand. It was just the way we were, aggressive and a handful, but we were as close as any brothers could be.

Mum had enough on her plate with Cathel and Graham being so young and she could have done without one of her kids constantly being in trouble, which was why she had to send Ian away to school. But all the changes meant there was a big void in my life. Dad had left and now Ian had gone too. The one good thing was that, at least for a time, I got closer to my mum than I ever had before. We were pretty much inseparable for a while and she was so loving and kind to be around. I also loved having more time to play with my little brothers. Graham was rough and tumble while Cathel was gentle and placid, as he would be all his life.

It was only when I started playing football at primary school that my life took a different direction. At the age of ten I became the first boy from our school to be selected for Plymouth Schoolboys. There was also a surreal experience that is completely at odds with the carnage that lay ahead. At Langley, our music teacher, Mrs Truscott, saw something in me that nobody else had spotted. We had been singing Christmas carols at the end of a lesson and she asked if I would stay behind for a couple of minutes. She called the headmistress in and then sat down at her piano.

'Listen to this,' she said to the head. 'Andrew,' she nodded, prompting me to begin.

She went through the scales on the piano and I followed them to perfection. I saw the teachers look at each other and smile and that was that; we finished and I went home. Apparently, I had the voice of an angel! I was going to be the next Aled Jones and the teachers were genuinely excited about my vocal ability. A week later, mum got a letter from school telling her that they wanted to put me forward for the Devon choir and would I be able to attend St Andrew's church in the city centre on Friday to demonstrate my singing ability? The problem was that the date of the recital coincided with my first game for Plymouth Schoolboys so that was the end of it. My singing career ended there and then but I have always wondered what might have happened if I had gone down that road because I would be anything but a choirboy in the years ahead.

Representing Plymouth Schoolboys meant that my dad – who was a decent amateur player himself and had turned out for the all-services team and Exeter City reserves on a few occasions – came to watch me whenever I played. I got to see more of him through football and, for a time, it was just him and me, which suited me down to the ground.

I liked Plymouth. It is so far off the beaten track that it often seems the world begins and ends there. It is of course strongly associated with the Royal Navy and seafaring generally and that appealed to me. I loved going down to Plymouth Hoe to watch the frigates, liners and oil tankers sail in and out of the harbour. The air was fresh and clean and it was also a hell of a lot warmer than Kinlochbervie.

We moved home again after a couple of years, this time to Peverel, which is not far from Plymouth Argyle's Home Park stadium. Aged eleven, I was enrolled at Southway comprehensive and that's where my problems really started. I was insolent to the teachers and forever getting into fights with the other pupils and it wasn't long before the head tactfully suggested I found another school. The problem was, whether it was Ian or with someone else, I loved fighting and couldn't help myself. The head told my mum he would rather not go through the process of expelling me and that a change of scenery might help. Either way, he made it clear that he didn't want me there anymore and so I moved to Burrington high school.

The problems didn't go away. I couldn't keep out of confrontations, mostly with older lads, and I continued fighting, trying to prove a point of some kind. It was just in me and from as far back as I could remember I'd been aggressive. Natural or otherwise, violence was just below the surface and it didn't take much to make me snap. I wasn't academic and didn't see the point of school, but when it came to football, I was a different animal; totally committed and focused. The football pitch was the one place I could be aggressive, but in a positive way. I also learned that it was the team that was important, not the individual. Winning was the be all and end all, not me proving I was the toughest kid on the block. The result was that I flourished and grew to become a pretty decent player.

I was also Plymouth Argyle daft and never missed a chance to watch them play. On Saturdays, Dad and I watched the first team and if there was a big crowd, he would haul me up on his shoulders for a better view. Tommy Tynan – a tough, no-nonsense striker from the old school of hard knocks – was my hero because he didn't take any shit from anyone. What with playing football for the school team and watching the Pilgrims I was as happy as I had ever been and totally absorbed in the city and in football. But, little did I know that my life was about to change forever. I was about to be hit with not one, but two, hammer blows.

When I decided to write this book, I agonised over whether I needed to talk about the first of those two incidents. Did it really matter? I finally decided the answer was yes. It has had a devastating effect on me and to leave it out would be wrong. I feel compelled to write about it.

It should never have happened. Not to me, not to anyone and certainly not to a lad who happened to be in the wrong place at the wrong time. I've managed to block it out of my head and even now it seems like a story I've been told about someone else, but it isn't.

It was 1982 and, as I did every other Tuesday night, I went along to watch Argyle reserves play their midweek fixture. It was cold and damp and Home Park would be freezing in the late autumn with icy winds blowing in from the sea. However, the weather wasn't going to put me off because this was one game that I really wanted to see. We were playing Crystal Palace reserves and Vince Hilaire, one of a crop of gifted black players emerging in England, was making his comeback from injury and I wanted to be there to see it. Hilaire was a bit special and I was fascinated by him, so I had my dinner, wrapped my green-and-white scarf around my neck and nipped out about six. Mum said to be home by half eight and no later. I cut through Central Park to get to the ground a bit quicker and got there in time for kickoff, paid my twenty-pence admission, bought some Bovril and stood shivering on the terrace with one hundred and fifty other diehards. I was in heaven. I was progressing well at schoolboy level so I reckoned I could be playing at Home Park myself in a few years if I kept it up. At least, that was my dream.

During the match Hilaire make one or two passes that set him apart from the rest and I reckoned that the ninety minutes of freezing my arse off had been worth it for those flashes of brilliance. As soon as the ref blew for full time, I wanted to get home and get warm. I had two ways of getting there: along Outland Road, which was well lit, but the long way; or across the park, which was pretty much pitch black by then, but would save me about ten minutes. As I was already late, there was only one choice: I jumped the park gate and off I went.

I could just about make the path out thanks to the street lighting flashing intermittently through the trees. I jogged along, playing out the game in my head and imagining what I would have done in certain situations. After a couple of minutes I came to a clearing, where I could make out the silhouette of the toilet block with the moon shining on the wet slates. That was good because I had my bearings and it wouldn't be much longer before I was back on the road. I was still in my own little world, turning over the ninety minutes of football in my head. Then, as I passed the toilets, a man's voice made me jump.

'Hey mate. Can you give me a hand?'

I was twelve, an innocent. If an adult asked for help I obliged. That's the way it works when you are a child. I walked towards the voice, whose owner had disappeared round the side of the toilet block.

'Just round here,' he said. I followed his instruction and then it all happened so fast. He grabbed me and then another bloke came out of nowhere and they dragged me into the toilets. It was pitch black inside and I was terrified. The door was slammed shut. I couldn't see either of them in the dark and after that it was a blur. I was beaten and then abused by them for what seemed like an eternity, but was more likely a couple of minutes. It ended when they quite casually walked out and disappeared into the darkness. There were no threats of what would happen to me if I made a noise or told anyone.

Nothing. I waited a few seconds before I left. I never screamed or shouted for help but I didn't look back. I was in shock but I managed to get home, still not believing what had just happened. I went upstairs, had a bath and went straight to bed. I didn't say a thing to mum. I couldn't.

I began sobbing during the night, unable to get it out of my head. Why the fuck had I stopped? Why didn't I think? Why hadn't I taken the main road home? I was always pushing it, taking a risk and thinking I was handy enough to look after myself. Why had it happened to me?

I couldn't go to school the next day, though mum thought I had. I had some breakfast, left the house, wandered around the shops for a bit and then went down to the Hoe. I just couldn't face class and being told what to do by a teacher. I was said to be the hardest lad in my year, and was the captain of Plymouth Schoolboys, so what was I to do? If I told anybody about what had happened and my mates found out, I don't think I'd have been able to face them again. So, until now, I decided never to tell a soul.

I wish I had told someone because things might have turned out different. Better still, I might have saved other kids from suffering a similar fate. I found out in later years other kids had been attacked in the same toilets so the chances are that the bastards who grabbed me were serial offenders. Back then, that was the last thing on my mind.

Somehow, within about three days, I managed to convince myself that none of it was real. I boxed it off and got it into my head that it had been a vivid nightmare. It was denial, I know, but the events of that night would occasionally be meted out in violent situations in the years to come. There were times I felt so desperate that the rage inside me was frightening. Subconsciously, I needed to settle the score, but, of course, it was a battle I could never win. There was to be no escape and my own mind became a prison cell, one that I felt I'd never break out of.

Back home, there was more upheaval. Mum told me she couldn't cope with the weekend fights and mayhem when Ian came home from school. It was too much for her. I was to move in with my dad – who had since remarried – initially for a few weeks. I felt a little hurt that I was being shipped out and no matter how much I loved Mum,

I tended to shut people out if I thought they didn't want me. That wasn't the case, but for a boy with a lot of issues, that's how I saw it.

From the moment I moved in, Dad made it clear that he wasn't going to put with any shit. Ian was still at boarding school so for the most part I was there on my own with Dad and his wife. Dad didn't pull any punches and he let me know what would happen if he started getting phone calls from school or visits from the police. Having him watch my every move was probably just what I needed and I enjoyed being in his company. He took me with him to the Barbican, a fishing quay in Plymouth harbour and an area littered with bars and pubs. I loved the environment, being on the quay, the smell of the sea and just being out with my dad.

We would go in the pubs together, play pool and have a laugh and I decided I wanted to stay with him on a permanent basis. I wasn't going back to Mum's. I got on okay with my step-mum, Margaret, but within a year they too had split up. As it was her house, we had to move into a two-bedroom, top-floor council flat in Stonehouse. The flat was a real shit-hole, but it didn't matter because we had somewhere of our own.

That we had a home at all was thanks to me, really, as Dad wouldn't have been entitled to anything if he had been a single man. However, as he had a thirteen-year-old son living with him, it literally opened one or two doors. Located behind Union Street – which is the heart of Plymouth's turbulent nightlife – Stonehouse wasn't a place for the faint-hearted. It was an area most residents who had anything about them were desperate to get away from. It was rife with gangs, drug pushers, prostitutes and a place the police had pretty much given up on. None of that bothered either me or my dad – we knew we'd be all right. It was ours and I loved it and felt comfortable there. We had our share of knocks on the door in the middle of the night, asking if we had any gear, but I'd just tell them to try across the landing and they'd go on their way.

I gradually went more to sea than to school. I would get up with Dad and go out on the boat with him at the crack of dawn, and I'd be out on the boats all day, returning at night. It suited me down to the ground. Fishing was in my blood and the school evidently didn't give a shit whether I was there or not, although I was nominally still a pupil until I was fifteen. I don't think they ever came looking for me or wrote enquiring about my whereabouts. They probably thought they were better off without a lad who was nothing but a pain in the arse to them.

Fishing and football – that was my life. Every weekend I played for my local club Elm United and we swept the board at amateur level, winning the league and cup year after year. I loved being around my dad all the time and I'd go with him and my older brother Ian and hang around the Barbican at the weekend. Dad liked to drink and he enjoyed a fight, too, so that's what we grew up around and I immersed myself in it. I felt alive in that environment and although I accept it's not how most parents would want their son to spend his time, it suited me down to the ground.

I saw plenty of punch-ups and other things a lad that age shouldn't see, which brings me to the second defining moment of my youth. It began over a game of pool. Dad thought he was next on the table and it led to an argument with two blokes I had never seen before. Dad would never back down. He got to the final of a major heavyweight boxing tournament when he was in the services and he was one of the hardest blokes in the city. So when he told me and my brother that he was going to sort it out, I knew what was coming and that it wouldn't be pretty. It never ended by talking things through; it couldn't with my dad. It needed to be settled with a straightener.

We went outside and within seconds Dad started fighting one of the guys he'd had the argument with. They went at it and, for once, Dad struggled. In fact, the other guy seemed to be on top and at that moment Ian said, 'Fuck this,' and ran across and kicked the guy Dad was fighting with in the head, sparking him out completely. He wasn't the type who would stand by and watch his old man getting leathered. The other guy jumped in and grappled with Ian before it fizzled out. I hadn't moved throughout. My feet were frozen to the ground.

Dad had taken a real beating and Ian had a few cuts and bruises to show for his efforts. I was relieved it was over and we walked home, initially in silence. Then, Dad looked at me and said, 'Look at the marks on your brother. Now look at you, you fucking coward. You've not got a mark on you.' He shook his head and carried on walking. For him, that was the end of it, but his words and the look on his face left me feeling empty. When your old man, the person you worship, calls you a coward, it's hard to take. I believed he was right and little did I realise that I would spend the rest of my life trying to prove to him and to myself that I wasn't.

The following morning, as far as Dad was concerned, it was as if nothing had ever happened. But I had spent the night replaying everything in my head. He was right. I had bottled it. How could I have stood there and not gone to help my dad and my brother? I felt like shit and his words kept echoing in my head.

'Now look at you, you fucking coward. You've not got a mark on you.'

I doubt if Dad even remembers what he said because the following morning he ruffled my hair and said, 'All right, son? What's for breakfast?'

He didn't realise his words had changed my life forever. Nobody was going to call me a coward again. I made a pact with the Devil. No amount of pain could hurt me more than the feelings I endured that night and I would never back down again for anyone or anything. Andy Morrison, a coward? No chance. I was having it, all day long. If trouble didn't come to me, I was going to go out and find it.

3

A Pilgrim's Dream

I had my first real drink when I was fourteen and it proved to be
something of a revelation. I was at a party with my mates and, as
the evening went on, I managed to down a two-litre bottle of cider
and the effect was, in hindsight, pretty scary. Apart from playing and
watching football and being on the fish quay with the lads, I never
felt I fitted in anywhere. I was uncomfortable with my own company
and I didn't mix well socially. I was shy, incredibly self-conscious and
always felt like I was on the outside looking in. The drink took all
that away and I felt fucking amazing. I had gone from Clark Kent to
Superman in the time it had taken me to down that bottle.

The booze cured me of my chronic shyness. I felt relaxed and
the world was a better place. Drink filled in the void in my life and
I knew from that moment on, I had something I could turn to when
I needed to blot out a memory or just feel better about myself. Of
course, I felt like shit the following morning and swore I would never
do it again and because I wanted to play football, I had enough inner
strength to leave drink alone for a while, but the seed had been firmly
planted in my mind.

Meanwhile, the scrapping never stopped. Ian and I wanted to be
like our dad and if we weren't knocking seven bells out of each other,
we would be involved with fights with gangs of lads from other areas.
We represented the fish quay and we'd take on gangs from Swilley or
Stonehouse and if it wasn't them, there were always the gypsies. They
always arrived during the summer and would be around Plymouth

for a couple of months, and, invariably, it would lead to numerous disputes or challenges being organised; just whatever it took to get a fight going.

There was plenty of banter down on the Barbican between the fishermen and the gypsies and talk must have turned at some point to this lad the gypsies reckoned was ready to take on anyone. He had battered several opponents in various challenges around the south-west and was reputed to be a handy fucker. Ian had just turned seventeen, while this lad was probably a year older, and, predictably, a bout was organised to find out who was the hardest. They must have been betting on the side because although there was local prestige involved, there had to be some other reason for the fight.

It wasn't long before the time and date had been agreed and a couple of days later we were on our way down to the fish quay to get it sorted. We found a place out of view of passers-by and Ian, me and a few of our mates stood watching as his opponent got himself psyched up by shadow boxing and screaming stuff to his mates and family. Ian said, 'Have you seen that prick? I'm gonna rip his fucking head off.' It was no big deal to him and it was unnerving how cool and calm he was. There must have been fifty spectators gathered round, with a circle left in the middle for the two fighters. Dad, loads of gypsies and a few fishermen plus other blokes I had never seen before were chatting among themselves, speculating about how it might turn out. It reminded me of a fight in the school playground, only this time nobody was going to stop the two protagonists.

Finally, the all-clear signal was given and Ian and his opponent squared up. Seconds later they were going at it. It was the first time I had seen what I would class as proper violence at close quarters and, with the adrenalin pumping, I loved it. I wanted to be in Ian's shoes, throwing punches and being in the centre of the crowd, even though they were baying for blood.

The other lad was bigger and initially got the better of Ian by getting on top of him and whacking him repeatedly. The air was charged and I felt it could kick off at any moment among the crowd if anyone stepped in to help either fighter but they continued uninterrupted. I was screaming at my brother to get up and, eventually, he started to come back into it until he finally managed to scramble up and pin his opponent down. Ian started ramming the guy's head down into the cobbles and there was blood everywhere. I wondered if he might actually kill him right before my eyes and the thing that worried me was I almost wanted him to because I felt as though I was in there with him, forcing the lad's head down onto the stone floor. Ian turned at one point and looked at my dad for a nod to say that was enough, but Dad just turned away. Ian carried on and slammed his opponent's head down a couple more times before looking up at Dad, who at last gave him a look that said, 'that'll do'.

The other lad somehow staggered to his feet and a few of his mates came over and helped clean him up. Then his dad came over, gave him a pat on the head and said, 'good effort, son'. And then everyone went off and had a drink together. There were neither any repercussions nor any animosity; everyone accepted the fight had gone the way that it had. Ian was now the top lad in the area and nobody could dispute it. I was proud of him and wanted to share in his euphoria and in his notoriety. But this was his time. I hoped mine would come before too long.

I also had other ambitions. I yearned to be a professional foot-baller, even though I had pretty much settled on being a fisherman in order to earn a living. I had all but dropped out of school, so it seemed the most natural thing in the world for me to follow in my old man's footsteps. We would get up at three in the morning, go down to the boat in the fish quay and sail ten miles offshore, out into Plymouth Sound towards the Eddystone lighthouse before putting the nets out, hoping for a good haul of skate and monkfish. We would bring in the catch, reset the nets and head back to the harbour.

We would make the same trip most days, although on a Saturday I got time off to play football for Elm United or Devon Schoolboys, who I had captained for a couple of years. I must have been doing something right because I received a letter from Southampton Football Club, inviting me to Hampshire for a week's training during half-term. We started out with a group of forty and then it was whittled down to maybe fifteen, of whom I was one. Southampton, a top-flight side at the time, invited me to join them on a two-week training course. They had players like Matt Le Tissier, Tim Flowers and Alan Shearer in the same age group as me, though obviously I hadn't a clue who they were at that time. However, as time passed, they were such fantastic talents that I soon learned their names. Through watching them train and their demeanour on and off the pitch, I quickly got an idea of the levels of dedication that were expected, even at that age. At night they would be talking about nothing other than football and whether or not they would be kept on as a YTS. I remember Shearer doing sit-ups by his bed before he turned in, such was his determination to make the best of himself. I absorbed it all and made a promise to myself that if I was signed on by a professional club, I would do things by the book, immerse myself totally and never be less than professional when it came to football.

I enjoyed my time with Southampton, but they didn't take me on. I was told I had made a good impression, and that they would be monitoring my progress, but that was a load of bollocks. Still, I didn't have to wait much longer before I landed the catch I really wanted. I got a phone call from a great bloke called Alec Brenton, who ran one of Plymouth Argyle's junior sides. He said the club had been keeping tabs on me for some time and he asked if I wanted to have a trial, which, of course, I almost bit his hand off to accept. Maybe the scout at Southampton had tipped him off, but, whatever the reason, I did really well in the trial game and was taken on by Argyle through a Youth Training Scheme. It was the proudest day of my life and I had to pinch myself that I would be wearing green and white for my job rather than as just a fan. Dad was pleased as punch but reminded me it was only the first step and that there was plenty of hard work ahead.

I look back on my YTS days as among the best of my life. The bond that the apprentices struck up was so strong that I'm still in contact with many of them to this day. Like all youngsters at football clubs we had to endure humiliation from time to time, such as when one of the first-team players, Nicky Law, decided we hadn't done enough running. So at the end of the session he summoned us over. We were on the edge of a big hill and he took out the balls and booted them over the fence and down into the brambles into a valley below. 'Go and get them you lazy fuckers and hurry the fuck up,' he barked. We scampered down the hill and came back with as many as we could find. It was like being a new recruit in the army; we were the lowest of the low.

Another time, a senior pro got one of the new apprentices to go into the toilet and warm the seat up before he had a shit. Imagine Didier Drogba doing that at Chelsea's academy! It was all done to establish a pecking order and we were under no illusions that we were at the bottom of the pile. The only way was up.

We used to play youth-team games on the training ground opposite Home Park, kicking off at one on a Saturday afternoon, prior to the senior team playing. After we had finished we would walk over to the stadium if we were at home, still dressed in our kit, and go through the away end to watch the big team. We got dog's abuse as we passed through the travelling fans, as you'd expect, but although a few of the lads were apprehensive, I loved it and wanted to wade into them.

That was a great time. I loved my club and was a fan first and foremost so I was literally living the dream. Plymouth was a tough, hard-drinking and, at times, unforgiving city, but I felt totally at home and now I had a real crack at making it as a professional footballer. It didn't get any better than that.

I was in luck, too, because there were some great pros at the club with the likes of John Uzzell, Lee Cooper and Kevin Hodges. Then of course there was my boyhood hero, the man I had grown up wanting to be: Tommy Tynan, the reigning club player of the year at the time I joined. For the first couple of months we would begin by training on our own and then join in with the first team. From time to time, I would be up against Tommy and I learned a lot from being around him because he was one of the most competitive men I have ever come across. Everything he was involved in, he had to win and if he couldn't win, he'd cheat. There was an incredible fire in him and I'll never forget the first time I played against him in training. The ball came towards Tommy but I jumped in ahead of him and cleared it upfield. Pleased with myself, I was about to turn and look at him, hoping for the approval of my hero. But all I got for my trouble was an elbow smashing into in my ribs.

'Hey, you little fucker,' he said in a thick Scouse accent. 'You don't come round me and the win the ball like that. Not now, not tomorrow, not ever. Understand?'

This was Tommy, my idol, talking to me and I was taken aback at first, but the fact remained that nobody did that to me and got away with it. Tommy had a real aura about him because of what he had done on and off the pitch. As a player he was an Argyle legend, and he always will be, but during training people gave him a wide berth. That wasn't just because he was the top man at Home Park; it was also down to his ferocious will to win, which even extended into practice matches. Teammates were also well aware that he could handle himself when the balloon went up. Where Tommy was concerned, they reasoned, it was always safer to back down.

But reputations meant fuck all to me. The next time a ball was played in – and you're probably ahead of me here – I launched him with a tackle that catapulted him into the air and he landed in a heap. This was a pivotal moment for us both because Tommy couldn't be seen to be challenged by a sixteen-year-old. He jumped up and grabbed me by my throat and would no doubt have had a swing if the other lads hadn't come over and pulled him back, telling him I was just a kid and that I hadn't meant it. Fucking right I had!

'I'll see you afterwards,' he said, trying to stare me out.

'Fine, I'll see you afterwards,' I told him. 'I'll meet you any fuckin' place you want. Let's do it now.'

He growled something under his breath and we carried on as before and, as it was, nothing happened and from that day forward there was mutual respect between me and Tommy. I didn't kick him and he didn't try to intimidate me if I got the better of him and that's how our relationship was, uneasy but respectful. So that was how my first session went. I had managed to lay down a marker and fall out with my idol, all within the space of thirty minutes! I later found out later that the older pros loved the fact someone had stood up to Tommy and that more than a few of them didn't care much for his ways.

A year later, aged seventeen, I had impressed sufficiently at youth and reserve levels to be included in the senior squad for the trip to play Aston Villa. Manager Dave Smith thought I was ready and I was included on the subs bench at Villa Park. They had some stellar names in their team with David Platt – who if memory serves me right was also making his debut – plus Garry Thompson and Tony Daley among the starting line-up. With sixty-five minutes on the clock, I was instructed to warm up because I was going on. I bounded down the touchline for a few minutes before the gaffer beckoned me back. This was what I had been waiting for so I took my tracksuit off and bounced up and down on the touchline, ready for my big moment. I played out the last twenty-five minutes, did all the right things and, although we lost the match 2–0, I was off and running. When I got back on the coach I was on a massive high, which was made even better because my old man had been there to see it, as he would be throughout my career.

When we got back to Home Park, everybody either drove home or was picked up, except for me. I got my bag, slung it over my shoulder and was just starting the walk home when the gaffer offered me a lift in his BMW 5-Series, which I gratefully accepted. Stewart Houston was in the front with Dave and we drove along the darkened backstreets of Stonehouse until we finally arrived at my block of flats. When the car stopped I saw them glance at each other, probably wondering where the fuck they were, or, more to the point, why one of their first-team players was living in a place like that. But I was fiercely proud of where I came from and I loved living there. It was a badge of honour, a this-is-who-I-am statement and to be honest I liked the notoriety that came with being a Stonehouse resident. Dave asked where my flat was and I pointed to the top right of the block. I knew what they were thinking, 'Fucking hell – what chance has a kid of making it coming from a shit-hole like this?'

'That's the best flat in the whole fucking block,' I insisted and they both laughed. I meant it too. I had laid my cards on the table. I had nothing to hide and they both knew exactly what they were dealing with.

I played just one more game that season – away to Millwall – and that proved to be another eventful afternoon. The Den was an intimidating place for any team to go to and the fact that it is located on Cold Blow Lane says it all. The stadium was dilapidated and dingy while their fans revelled in their reputation as the most feared in the country. That meant fuck all to me and I was relishing the match, no matter what the home support threw at me, though I have to admit they got one over on me. I may have been a bit too cocky because a few of their fans shouted me over as I went out to warm up and, as an act of bravado, I went over to hear what they had to say. As I got within a few yards, one of them squirted me with ketchup and then I got tea, beer and fuck knows what else chucked over me. They started laughing and shouted 'Millwall, Millwall, Millwall,' at me. I was covered in crap but I suppose I asked for it. I had stuck my head in the lion's den and paid the price for my naivety. I had put the 'green' in Green Army, but I didn't let it get me down.

Facing the great Teddy Sheringham I had a decent game and in one challenge I launched him into the air with a hard but fair tackle. I remember Mick McCarthy, the Millwall centre half, coming across and picking me up from behind. I spun around and was right in his face. The other Argyle lads were saying, 'calm down for fuck's sake,' but we were away to Millwall and there was no way I was going to leave without making an impression. It needed to be done and although I picked up a booking, I walked off at the end of the game with my chest out and my head held high. I glanced over to where those fuckers had been standing, but they had gone. Good job, too, because I was so pumped up that I felt ready for anything. The Millwall players and fans might not have appreciated my robust style, but the travelling Argyle fans loved it and over the next twelve months I forged a fantastic relationship with them. They knew I was one of them because word had got out that I used to stand on the Devenport End before I started playing for the club and they loved that. It wasn't long before the first chants of 'Psycho, Psycho' were shouted in my direction, but I was no Stuart Pearce. I played the game in a similar style to him, with honest, controlled aggression and no more, but you know how fans are and had I been on the terraces watching someone like me, I would have chanted the same thing.

They also loved the fact that I didn't care about reputations. The bigger they were, the harder they fell as far as I was concerned. When I was in the tunnel before a game, I was a warrior and the pitch became the Thunderdome. If somebody got in my way or thought they could intimidate a raw teenager, they were in for a surprise. I had so much aggression and adrenalin pumping around my system that before a game I'd go into the toilet and head butt a door. I was so keyed up I felt ready to explode. At Millwall I had given Terry Hurlock, their hardest player, as good as I got and at home to Portsmouth the following season, I went one better by nailing their top man during the game. For obvious reasons the match is known as the dockyard derby and it means a lot to both the fans and the players. Pompey were a decent side at the time and I was looking forward to the challenge. We lined up alongside them in the Fratton Park tunnel and Martin Kuhl and Warren Aspinall were to my left. They both looked at me and started laughing at me because I had Vaseline on my eyebrows and was bouncing on my toes in preparation for walking out.

'Look at that fucking clown, he looks like he's going into a boxing ring,' Kuhl sniggered. They both started mimicking me and generally taking the piss, but while older pros got away with that when I was an apprentice, those days were long gone. I would get my own back on the pitch. Late in the game Pompey won a free-kick and I lined up in the wall in front of our goal. Kuhl joined it, with the intention of forcing a gap when the kick was taken. We jostled for a moment and the shot sailed over our bar and into the crowd. This was my chance. I quickly looked round and saw that the ref had his back to me as he made his way back up the pitch. I walked alongside Kuhl before lamping him in the face, splitting his lip up to his nose. I had caught him cold and he went down in a heap clutching his face. Then, after about a minute, he got up and came after me as I was jogging backwards to the halfway line.

'Is that the fucking best you've got is it?' he asked.

I smiled at him. 'No, but it was enough to put you down so if I fucking hit you right you'll be on your way to casualty.'

He didn't bother me again.

There was another time we played Leeds and I was up against David Batty and Vinny Jones and although nothing in particular happened, I was more than comfortable in their presence because I wouldn't have thought twice about getting involved if anything had cropped up. There was no way a young kid should have felt like that and I had no right to be that confident, but nothing fazed me. I had made the choice never to back down and had the confidence to back it up.

It was incredible that I was doing so well because I was still living something of a double life as a fisherman, helping my dad on a regular basis. Perhaps inevitably there was one occasion when the two worlds collided, well almost. It was the day of a match but I still got up at half-three in the morning to put my wellies and oilskins on in readiness to go out on the boat. We landed a decent catch at the fish quay about eight o'clock but then I had to get ready to travel to our match at Brighton, with the team bus leaving Home Park just two hours later. I went back to the flat as quickly as I could to change but there was a slight problem: I had forgotten my fucking keys. Time was running out and I had no choice but to hurriedly make my way to the ground in a taxi, in full knowledge that if the gaffer saw me turn up dressed as a fisherman, I'd be in deep shit. The coach was outside the front entrance with the engine idling so I sneaked around the back of the ground in hope of finding the kitman, but he was nowhere to be seen. Luckily, there was a woman in the laundry washing some kit and after I explained what had happened, she sorted me out with a tracksuit and trainers. After a quick shower I was on the coach and ready to go. Hard to imagine many players doing that these days, but that's how I lived my life in those days. I was up against Mark McGhee that night and had a good game during a 1–1 draw so my extra-curricular activities hadn't affected me that much.

Not long after that, I was offered my first professional contract with Argyle. I had served my apprenticeship and had earned a crack at making a career for myself. I was of course grateful to Dave Smith for having faith in me. He was a charismatic guy and a terrific gaffer. Nicknamed 'The Ciderman' by the fans, for reasons that escape me, he had been selling insurance for more than a year, at which point he successfully applied for the Plymouth job. He was a fellow Scot who hadn't had much of a playing career but had guided both Mansfield Town and then Southend from division four to promotion. He joined Argyle part-way through the 1984/85 season, winning promotion in his first full campaign. He was old school and he evidently saw something in me that he liked. Stewart Houston was a really good coach, well ahead of his time in his training techniques and sessions and he improved my game no end while he was at Home Park. However, after the pair guided Argyle to their highest finish for many years – seventh in the old second division, then the second tier of English football – Smith decided to return to Scotland to manage Dundee at the end of the 1987/88 campaign and Houston left, too.

The board turned to former Norwich manager Ken Brown and I now had to knuckle down again and impress him, as of course did the whole squad. I was mainly playing reserve-team football, with the odd senior game thrown in every now and then. I was doing really well for the stiffs, but Brown only gave me the occasional run out. I like to think I didn't let him down when called upon, but I was still nowhere near a regular starting place in the first eleven. That's what I wanted and, being a cocky fucker, felt I deserved. I was never less than professional and totally committed when I played and trained and, apart from the odd flashpoint, I was steady and reliable.

I liked Brown. He was a decent guy but he only lasted eighteen months before being sacked. The revolving manager's door at Home Park showed no signs of rusting over with high expectations placed on whoever took on what was something of a poisoned chalice. The level of investment in the playing squad simply wasn't good enough and the board had an itchy trigger finger so I wasn't that surprised or, in truth, that disappointed to see him go.

John Gregory stepped into the void on a temporary basis while the board decided who they wanted to take the club forward. It was an awkward time for me because I had been in talks about a new contract and I wasn't sure whether to wait until the new man came in or to speak to Gregory about it. I didn't have an agent, but my one experience of having representation – if you could call it that – had been enough to put me off for life. I decided I would seek advice from Gregory, who put me on to a London-based agency run by one of his friends. The manager told me they would look after me and make sure I got the best financial package when it was time to sit down and start talking. So when mine and Martin Barlow's contracts were up, we both went with the agent Gregory had recommended.

In the meantime another former Argyle legend, Dave Kemp, took over as manager and an agent was assigned to meet him and discuss new deals for me and Mark. In my view he really chanced his arm, because he marched into the gaffer's office and said, 'Right, I want £600 a week for these lads plus a £20,000 signing on fee each.' Kempy laughed, suggested he was delusional and told him to fuck off out of his office because the meeting was over. The guy disappeared back to London and Kempy called me in and asked me what I was looking for. Kempy's problem was that the agent had wanted to make me and Mark the highest-paid players at the club, something that wasn't going to happen. I told him I hadn't a clue what my representative asked for because he hadn't even talked to me, so I gave him a figure I was happy with.

'Give me five minutes,' Kempy said. When he came back into the office he told me, 'Yeah, we can do that for you.' That taught me I didn't need anyone to fight my corner – I never have – and I resolved to handle my own affairs in future. There was a sting in the tale, however. Later that evening I got a call from the guy who owned the agency saying how happy he was that one of his lads had got me a new deal. 'He did fuck all,' I insisted. 'He was thrown out of the office and I sorted it out myself, so thanks for nothing.' I put the phone down and that was that, or so I thought.

Two days later an invoice arrived for £1,400 for the renegotiation of my contract. Cheeky fuckers! I spoke to the PFA who told me the bill was correct and legally watertight and there was nothing I could do about it because I had signed an agreement with the agency. I had to pay up and shut up, which didn't sit too well with me, but it taught me an important lesson about checking the small print before signing anything. Maybe on one or two occasions I could have got better deals, but in all honesty, it wasn't the most important part of football for me. I wanted a manager who wanted me to play for him because that meant more to me than any pay packet or bonus and I was about to get exactly that.

I immediately took to Dave Kemp and after he had canvassed the opinions of those in the know at the club, he put me right back into the team. Apparently, more than one of those he spoke to about me had told him, 'Get young Morrison back in. He's just what we need.' Because of the faith he showed in me, I immediately felt indebted to him. I was going to show him he had made the right decision. Kempy was great with me in so many ways. He invested plenty of time in me on the training ground, encouraging me to think more deeply about my role in the team and how I could improve my game.

We were in twentieth position but there was still time to save ourselves from the drop. In Dave's first game in charge, I had a fucking stormer at centre half and we were 3–0 up against Sunderland at half-time, so things couldn't have gone much better. He came in the dressing room afterwards and said, 'The way forward for this football club is young lads like Morrison.' That was all I needed to hear.

We lost only five of our last sixteen games. And we were even better in the last eight games, in which we were unbeaten, finishing in sixteenth place, well out of danger. Things also went well on a personal level and I managed to score the winning goal with a thumping header against Ipswich Town during the run in.

I had finally got my first-team shirt. I wasn't going to give it up without a fight.

4

Nightmare on Union Street

Up to the age of seventeen, I'd say my drinking was no worse than any other lad in my peer group. I drank when I was out with mates, and had a good time, but it was more social boozing than anything else. I began to drink heavily when I turned eighteen and started going out regularly with my brother Ian on Union Street or to the bars down by the fish quay. Initially, it wasn't affecting my football, but there were times when it did and it was no coincidence that it was around this time that I started getting in trouble with the police and the hierarchy at the club. More often than not, a night out with Ian ended in violence of some sort. He was an outstanding fighter and it was in his blood to have a regular scrap.

I didn't stand by watching when he kicked off and I got caught up in countless brawls, willingly, it's worth adding. Somehow I managed to avoid ending up in a cell, through luck more than anything else, but it was just a matter of time before events caught up with me and, when they did, the proverbial shit hit the fan.

One Saturday night after a home game I went out and was on the lash with some mates until the early hours, when a few of us drifted off for a kebab. It didn't take much to flick my switch when I'd been on the piss – it was always half-pressed at the best of times – and any opportunity to kick off was accepted with relish. After we had eaten our kebabs we were waiting in line for a taxi and words were exchanged with another group of lads stood in front of us. One got a bit lippy, took it too far and I ended up smacking him in the face.

That, I reckoned, was the end of it and I thought no more about it because it was happening every weekend by then. Somehow I had allowed it to become the norm.

I turned up for training on the Monday morning and Dave Kemp called me into his office and told me the police wanted me to go down to the station because of an incident at the weekend. 'Some bloke got his nose broken,' Kempy said with his eyebrows raised, questioningly. When he had asked the police what I needed to take with me they replied, 'Try a solicitor.' It had been coming.

I went along to the station with a brief the club sorted for me and I was charged with assault and actual bodily harm, my first proper 'adult' charge. I was told I would have to appear a few months later at a pre-trial, at which witness statements were assessed in order to determine if there was enough evidence to secure a conviction. Ultimately, there wasn't and the case was thrown out, though the only reason I had been tracked down in the first place was because I had been recognised. I could no longer fly below the radar in my hometown. I had played enough games for my face to become known and I was appearing on the back pages of newspapers on a regular basis, which of course brought me to the attention of the public. I should have been keeping a low profile but I refused to learn my lesson.

Kempy read me the riot act and said that if I wanted a career in football, this could never happen again. I made all the right noises and swore that I would stay on the straight and narrow, the first of many such promises I made during my career. All well and good, except that the following Saturday I was out on the town with Ian and a few mates from the Barbican, all scrappers. Every one of them was looking for trouble and, if they didn't find trouble, it found them. On this particular evening, however, things took a decidedly nasty turn.

There was a rival group of lads who drank in Plymstock that we'd had a number of skirmishes with in the past and it had been threatening to go off with them for months. This night we decided to bring things to a head. There were eight of us and ten of them and I was well up for it. I gave no thought either to potential repercussions or to the fact that I had only narrowly avoided a prison term; I was enjoying myself too much to care. As it happened, their top lad and

Ian decided to have a set-to on their own and went to a pool room at the back of the pub where they began fighting. They must have been at it for a good five minutes before Ian started to get on top and eventually gave this guy a real battering. It felt inevitable it would kick off between the rest of us at any minute, but for some reason it didn't so we left and headed back to Union Street. We were all singing and having a great time, with the adrenalin in full flow, and were about to go into a pub we often hung out in to finish the night off.

Then, in a flash, it was mayhem.

Out of the corner of my eye I saw someone run from behind a parked car; it was the guy Ian had given a pasting earlier on. He ran up to Ian and stuck a pint glass in his face, cutting his eye, nose and forehead open. There was claret everywhere. His assailant was gone as quickly as he had appeared and with the element of surprise in his favour he had put one over on us. He had obviously lost face in front of his mates and wanted to make Ian pay for the humiliation he had suffered. We got Ian off to hospital where they removed the glass and then he underwent plastic surgery. But I knew my brother was going to be scarred for life. There's an old saying, 'If you live by the sword, you die by the sword,' and it's so true. What happened to Ian was the harsh, but inevitable, consequence of living on the edge. Getting hurt was almost an occupational hazard.

I had a game for Argyle on the following Tuesday and it was decided that we would even things up after I had taken care of business on the pitch. The lad who had done my brother wasn't going to get away with it and this time we would take out his whole crew to teach him a lesson. We knew his mates played pool on a Wednesday evening so we got tooled up with baseball bats, crowbars and coshes, jumped into two transit vans and headed for Plymstock. The rush was unbelievable. We were fully charged and ready to take them and the pub apart. We were egging each other on as if we were about to parachute into enemy territory and when we got there we jumped out of the vans, ready for anything. It was comical. We burst in, shouting, 'Come on you fuckers. Let's fuckin' have it,' only to find a little old bloke supping his pint in the corner. It turned out the pool team were away from home that night! We stood there looking at one another, unsure of what to do next and I suddenly snapped out of the daze I'd been in. The consequences of what we were about to do suddenly became clear. 'Thank fuck they aren't here,' I thought. What we had planned was organised violence, a conspiracy involving some heavy-duty weapons. We could have been looking at a lengthy prison term for grievous bodily harm or even attempted murder.

That episode ended with the correct legal procedures being followed. The police traced the guy who glassed Ian and because it had been captured on closed-circuit television, he was convicted and sent to jail. Ian didn't help the police with their enquiries, nor did he give evidence against his assailant in court. He knew it came with the territory, even though the guy had crossed the line. Getting involved in things like that was madness, total madness, and it still staggers me that I let it happen. But although I had enough sense not to become embroiled in gang warfare after that, I had no desire to change the way I was living. Quite simply I was having too much of a good time. I wanted it all. I wanted to train during the week, play on a Saturday afternoon, go out on the lash with my pals and then begin the whole cycle again. The majority of fans at Argyle knew what I was like away from football because word soon gets around. However, because I did the business on the pitch a blind eye was turned to my nocturnal activities.

The beauty of being in Plymouth was that nobody knew me outside of the city and so my bad-boy reputation stayed in the city. Nobody came to Plymouth unless they had to or were passing through. If I had been a player in London or Manchester nobody in football would have come anywhere near me because my misdemeanours would have been plastered across the front pages. It was thanks to Plymouth's isolation that I thrived as a player and progressed unhindered. The local press seemed to ignore to my shenanigans, too, and with no real television coverage of the lower leagues in the late 1980s, and no internet or mobile-phone footage of me causing mayhem in a bar posted on YouTube, I carried on doing whatever the fuck I wanted and more often than not got away with it. That wouldn't happen today.

A saving grace was that one thing in my life was going well. I had begun seeing a girl called Paula, who would eventually become my wife. I met her at an Argyle match because her sister was married to John Uzzell, one of my teammates, and she was a regular at Home

Park. It didn't take long for her to fall for my charm and good looks! We were the same age and hit it off from the first moment we met. In general, I behaved when I was around her. She was a good influence and she accepted me for who I was, warts and all. However, there was nothing she could do once I was out on the town with the drink inside me. I was being totally irresponsible and it was only a matter of time before the train hit the buffers. To my eternal shame Paula was a passenger on that train and ended up getting hurt.

One night I was out with Paula, Ian, my dad and a few friends on a pub crawl. We had a few drinks on the fish quay before heading to Union Street to find a late-night drinking hole. Nobody in their right mind went on Union Street late on a Saturday night unless they were too far gone to care, or looking for a fight. There was a place called the Octagon that was sprinkled with dodgy pubs and strip clubs. We found a pub, had a few drinks and carried on enjoying ourselves. But as the booze flowed the mood darkened; we became argumentative and tetchy. Then one of our group bumped into some sailors at the bar. I don't know if he did it on purpose or not but it didn't matter. It went off. My dad, Ian and I were in the thick of it and there was broken glass flying around and furniture getting wrecked. Dad was laying out people all over the shop and Ian and I were his very able lieutenants. The fighting spilled onto the street and as we emerged from the pub still scrapping away both Dad and I had our tops ripped off. There was another surprise: we found ourselves staring down the lens of a television camera. A crew was filming a documentary about the lawlessness on Union Street. From their point of view, it couldn't have been timed any better, whereas for me, it couldn't have been timed any worse. At the time I didn't appreciate how much trouble I was in because I now had another big problem: Paula's leg had been gashed in the melee. Understandably, I didn't pay the camera crew any attention and instead I tended to Paula and then helped her into an ambulance.

The following Monday, I was half-watching BBC's *Look South West* while I ate my dinner, when I recognised a bar on Union Street and turned up the volume. Then the screen showed a drunk, stripped to the waste, staggering all over the street. It was Plymouth Argyle footballer Andy Morrison, not that the reporter knew that or mentioned me by name. But there I was in all my glory, larger than life and twice as ugly. I was screwed. The television crew had been tipped off there was a fight in one of the pubs nearby and were on hand just as we were leaving. Dad and I looked as though we had been in a cage fight and Paula's leg was covered in blood. If I had wanted to land myself in deeper shit I couldn't have scripted it better. As they filmed the ambulance pulling away, the voiceover came on: 'And it is young girls like that who are the innocent victims of these nights of mindless violence. . . . '

Within a few minutes the phone was ringing off the hook asking if that had been me on the news? I thought, 'Shit, here we go again.' How fucking stupid could I be? I was going to have to face the music yet again because there was no way this wouldn't get back to the gaffer. Sure enough, the following day, the inevitable happened and I was called in to see Kempy. If I hadn't been pulling my weight on the pitch, I would have been shown the door, but I was one of Argyle's best players and if the club did decide to get rid of me they would have got a healthy transfer fee. With finances at the club the way they were, they weren't in a position to sack me and wave goodbye to a few hundred grand.

Actually, that's something I've grown to hate about football over the years. They should treat footballers the same as people in any other profession so that when you step out of line, you're treated accordingly. Kempy had invested a lot of time in me, given me some wonderful advice and moved me into midfield and I was really coming on as a player but they'll only get rid of you it suits them, not because it's the right thing to do. If you're worth anything, they'll fine you and suspend you but if you happen to be rotting in the reserves on a fat contract when you get into trouble, you'll be gone in a flash – ask Dennis Wise because in my view that's what happened to him at Leicester City. They were desperate to get rid of him so when he breached club discipline, he made it easy for them. When clubs do nothing, they're condoning your behaviour, no matter what fines or suspensions they hand out, and that's exactly what Argyle were doing in this instance. So I got another warning, effectively a slap on the wrist.

Despite the club's leniency I had a deep-rooted problem. My drinking was out of control and, by the time I turned twenty-one, I already had pronounced alcoholic tendencies. It was a desperate situation to be in and maybe if I'd sought, or been forced to get, help I could have got on top of things. Every time I drank, it was to get out of my tree and at the same time I began to recognise there was a real rage in me that was leading to increasingly violent episodes. I have no doubt it was the drink that reawakened all the old insecurities and fears I had harboured for the past ten years. I had never come close to dealing with what had happened to me in the park. I had never spoken about it to anyone; I just blanked it out. At least I thought I had. The devastating effect of Dad calling me a coward had lain dormant, too, but rather than time solving those issues, they had festered like a rotting carcass. Alcohol was the key that unlocked the door I never wanted to open when I was sober. It let a demon loose. It came out of the fucking pits of the earth and waited for the right moment to start chipping away and however hard I tried to quieten the voices mocking me, the more it haunted me. My only escape was booze, and then brawling. Such was the rage and resentment that on a night out, the smallest thing could set me off. If a doorman told me to wait for a moment, I'd consider it too good an opportunity to turn down. I was forever chasing something that would quell the rage within, but the reality was nothing ever could. I'm not saying I was like that all the time, but if conditions were right bad things happened, putting my career at risk with every punch I threw and head-butt that connected.

I went on a bender one Saturday and turned up for training the following day, still half pissed. I passed Kempy in the corridor without making eye contact and headed for the changing rooms to be sick. I never made it, blacking out as I went through the door and then smashing my head on the team bath. I was taken to hospital where I was cleaned up and given ten stitches in a gash on my forehead. I went back to the club at lunchtime and was told to report to the gaffer to explain what had happened. It was a Sunday, and we had a game on the Tuesday, and he told me if I wasn't fit for selection, I would be fined. I did play – there was never a doubt in my mind that I wouldn't – but I wore a bandage round my head and had a good game by all accounts. That was my quandary. Whatever I did it didn't seem to affect my game. It might have been better if it had.

There was a real drinking culture at Argyle in those days, as there was throughout football. Kenny Brown, David Byrne, Nicky

Marker and Shaun McCarthy – 'The Tuesday Club' – were all fond of the booze and after training on a Tuesday afternoon we would have some unbelievable drinking sessions. It was an accepted part of the game and it bonded the lads together, although it was the wrong environment for a twenty-one-year-old who was already struggling to control his drinking. The problem was I never really stood out from the crowd. I went just a little bit further than the others and so I never thought I had a major problem. Football, drink, violence. It was a vicious circle. On one side there was a promising professional footballer and on the other there was an alcoholic with no self-control. The paths ran in parallel but there were many more times when they crossed, with explosive results.

Argyle's hooligan firm was known as The Central Element, or TCE, and on one night out, Ian intentionally wound a couple of them up, and ended up giving one of their mob a beating. Word got out about what he'd done and it led to their guy keeping out of his way and Ian not drifting on to their patch. Nevertheless it led to a long-standing feud that rumbled on for years.

It wasn't long before the feud with the TCE exploded into violence. Our younger brother, Graham, had just come home on leave from the army. He had joined up straight from school and was eager to celebrate completing basic training. He was only seventeen but probably considered himself to be a man, and a man who could handle himself. He was desperate to go for a few pints with his older brothers, despite the fact that Dad wanted him to steer clear of trouble.

'I don't want him going down town with you two,' he told us over a drink at the fish quay. 'He's too young and he doesn't need all that shit. Let him find it himself if that's what he wants to do, but don't take him to it. Keep him out of it.'

A week or so later Graham had been pleading to go to the pub so we just laughed, ruffled his hair and took him with us, against Dad's wishes, but, we reasoned, what he didn't know couldn't harm him. We looked after our little brother, he had a great night and the next day Dad said that as long as he didn't get into any trouble it was all right for him to go with us every now and then.

Of course, it was all going to end in tears and the following weekend, it did. I played for Argyle in the afternoon and later met up with some mates and Graham. We stayed on the Barbican for a while before moving to Union Street. It was in one of its many pubs that the inevitable happened. Ian, Graham, me and a couple of other lads got into an argument with some of The Central Element. By the time the doormen came in and separated us, it had blown over and me and my brothers jumped in a taxi and had a good laugh about the short-lived scrap. The adrenalin was pumping and our clothes were torn and dishevelled. I asked Graham if he was okay.

'Yeah, great. Fucking fantastic,' he replied. Then my stomach turned when I saw he had half his ear missing. Somebody had bitten it off in the brawl but nobody had noticed at the time. Ian and I weren't thinking, 'Fuckin' hell. Our little brother has just lost half his ear.' It was more, 'Shit. Dad's going to kill us and we're both for the fucking high jump.'

We sped to the hospital where Graham underwent plastic surgery. They took a piece from the back of his ear and patched things up as best they could. I was half-hoping he could lie low for a few days and then head back to training camp so that Dad wouldn't find out. Ian could then dismiss it as a fight that had taken place somewhere else. After I finished a training session the following Monday, Ian and I mustered the courage to come clean to Dad. We might have been fearless when we were out on the lash, but our old man scared the shit out of us. He was a giant of a man, bigger than us in every sense and he had hands like shovels. We headed down to the fish quay to see him but our attempts to smooth things over were in vain. He had already spoken to Graham and the look of utter contempt he gave us will stay with me till the day I die.

'You don't fucking learn, do you?' he growled. 'Get out of my sight. I don't want to see either of you.'

There was an air of menace about Dad that convinced us we should stay out of his way for a while. He didn't speak to us for weeks and, of course, he was right. In recent years I have often reflected that it was fucking mental that the lads we fought with that night were the ones I ran to celebrate with when we scored on a Saturday afternoon. There are lots of things I'm not proud of in my life and the incident with Graham summed up everything about my world back then, both good and bad.

Things were slowly changing for me at Argyle and not for the better. In fact they went rapidly downhill, both on and off the pitch. We hadn't carried on our form from the end of the previous campaign and we had been in the bottom four for the best part of five months. In February 1992, inevitably, Kempy paid the price with his job. I was devastated because he had given me my chance, had always encouraged me and helped to develop me as a player. And of course he had forgiven me every time I fell off the wagon. In consequence, I thought very highly of him. He was honest enough to let me know that scouts had been watching me and that what I needed to do was to get a move to a bigger club. Spurs, Derby County and Wolves had all expressed an interest, apparently, but it hadn't taken any of them much digging to find out that I came with a truckload of baggage.

I was choked when I was told that Kempy had been sacked and I think if I could have gone at the same time, I would, but I stayed on at Home Park, at least in the short term. I couldn't imagine any of the clubs Kempy had mentioned had put in a bid for my services because the board would have snapped their hand off.

A new chairman arrived shortly thereafter in the shape of Dan McCauley and he put a bit of money into the club. If he had come in sooner and given the funds to Kempy, I think he would have turned things around because the lads loved him and we weren't a million miles from being a decent team. Instead, we got Peter Shilton as player-manager, with John McGovern as his number two. Nobody could argue with their pedigree or their standing in the game and the lads wondered whether they would use that experience positively, to instil belief into us individually and as a team.

But Shilton got off to a terrible start with the lads. When he introduced McGovern to the squad he said: 'I want you to show him the same respect you to show me. Remember, he's lifted the European Cup, something that none of you will ever do so don't forget that.' We were taken aback by his remarks and we looked at each other open mouthed. What there was to gain by putting us down like that? There wasn't a hint of humour; to me he was so fucking wooden that I wondered if he had ever been mistaken for a door.

It was a gamble to change manager mid-season, but sometimes it pays off, sometimes it doesn't. Shilton quickly assessed the squad in his first few sessions and moved me back into central defence. I had filled out a lot and, in terms of my physique, centre back was where I belonged, so I had no problem with it. I couldn't have got off to a much better start under Shilts either, scoring in his first game in charge against his former club Derby County. It should have been the platform we needed to kick on, and a 1–0 win over Bristol City in our next game moved us out of the bottom three, but it wasn't long before the impetus faded and we began to struggle again.

I never took to Shilton, perhaps because Kempy was such a tough act to follow, or maybe it was because he just had an air about him I didn't like. I don't think Shilton ever got what Plymouth Argyle, its supporters or its people were about. We were an underachieving second-tier side with a passionate fan base, but he seemed to think he was still in the first division and playing for England. Worst of all, he just couldn't hide it. Despite everything he had achieved in the game and his wealth of experience, I don't think he had much respect for the lads and based on the way he spoke to us and his body language I got the impression he looked down on us. In fact, I'm fucking certain of it.

And to me he always played to the gallery on match days, which also wound the lads up. He would make all these wild hand gestures during the game, which went way over the top and made it obvious that he didn't think we were good enough. At least, that's how we saw it. If a shot went over the bar he would turn to the fans behind him and throw his arms up in despair and shake his head. We were well aware of what he was doing. Everything about him was transmitted to the squad in a completely negative way and it told on the pitch.

The only chance I got for a little payback was during warm-ups, when he went in goal. I used to smash the ball at him from fifteen yards and I'm surprised he didn't stick me up front given the amount of shots that whistled past his head. He made a decent target, I'll give him that. A lot of the lad were overawed by him, but I challenged him constantly; at training, during matches and in team talks. Anyone would have thought I didn't like the guy.

We still had a chance of staying up going into our last game, despite the unrest in the dressing room. All we had to do was to beat Blackburn and Oxford United would go down instead of us, but we were well beaten on the day, losing 3–1. It was a huge blow for Argyle and the city, too. A place the size of Plymouth deserved to be pushing for the top flight, not facing up to away days at Colchester and Exeter. The only thing we could do was to buckle down and get back up at the first time of asking.

Shilts strengthened the squad in the summer, bringing in Warren Joyce, Paul Dalton and Steve Castle for £200,000 apiece, as well as Gary Poole, and we were all set to give it a real go in the new season. There was a better atmosphere when we returned after the summer and during pre-season training. The new lads started calling me Jake, which I let go for a few sessions until I wondered if it wasn't some sort of piss take. I corrected them every time, telling them my nickname was Jock, but it carried on until I decided to have a private word with the next person who called me Jake. I pulled Gary Poole to one side and told him, 'Look pal, its Jock, not Jake. Everyone knows me as Jock in Plymouth. Okay?'

'Oh we know that,' he said. 'We're calling you Jake after Jake La Motta in *Raging Bull*.'

I said I had never heard of La Motta or *Raging Bull*. He told me it was a movie starring Robert Di Niro – who plays a ferociously competitive middleweight boxer – and that I should watch it because it reminded the new lads of me. That night, I rented the video from my local store and finally understood what they were on about. I accepted Jake or Jock from that point on as I assumed it was a back-handed compliment.

The season proved to be tough as we struggled to adapt to life in the third tier. At least off the field things were going well, with Paula discovering she was pregnant a month or so into the new campaign. I was high as a kite and couldn't believe I was going to be a dad. With a baby on the way it also made me realise I had to get my future sorted out, but the problem was that neither the club nor Shilton were knocking my door down with the offer of a new contract.

We were never going to go up after the start we made and we floated around mid-table with Shilton unable properly to motivate us. Home life wasn't easy, either, as Paula was having a difficult pregnancy and was confined to bed for six weeks with preeclampsia, but, thankfully, less than twenty-four hours after a 1–0 home defeat to Port Vale, our first child, Arron, entered the world. The little rascal gave us the fright of our lives because he stopped breathing for a few seconds after he was born and I could tell there was something wrong because of the way the nurses were rushing around. To our great relief, within a matter of minutes everything was back to normal and I held my son for the first time. Not surprisingly, and for once with good reason, all I wanted to do was get down the pub and celebrate his birth.

I went out against Stoke City a week later feeling I could take on the world and with Paula in good health and back home with the baby, I wanted to end the season on a high. I did what I could, but we lost the game, pretty much summing a disappointing season in which we finished in fourteenth place. Regardless of what I thought about Shilton as a man, on the pitch I never gave less than 100 per cent. The fans must have agreed with that assessment because I was runner up in Argyle's player-of-the-season awards. I was waiting to be called in for the new contract I had been promised earlier in the year, but the phone didn't ring. I had been told I would be given a new deal worth £450 a week – the same as the new guys were on – plus a £30,000 signing-on fee. But Shilton held back for some reason, which pissed me off no end.

The local paper picked up on the story and suggested Dan McCauley and Shilton were at loggerheads over me. At the same time the fans were making it clear they weren't happy that my contractual situation hadn't been resolved. Finally, a few weeks before pre-season training started, the chairman contacted me and said that he was going to offer me a three-year deal worth £500 per week, with a £15,000 signing-on fee. He had evidently taken matters into his own hands and decided he wanted me to stay. It wasn't as much as I had hoped for but, still, it gave me the perfect opportunity to rub Shilton's nose in it because of the way he had handled things. If he had wanted rid of me, he should have been up front and said as much to my face, but instead he let me stew at a time when I needed a bit of security. I couldn't resist giving him a call to let him know what the chairman had offered and that I was going to accept it.

'Just hold fire before signing anything,' Shilton said.

'Why?' I asked.

'Just give me until this evening.'

I knew he didn't want me at the club and that he had plans to bring someone else in. Quite clearly, our relationship, such as it was, had deteriorated to the point where he didn't want to work with me any longer. That suited me fine, but it still meant I had no new deal sorted. Something was going on, but because I didn't have an agent, I was out of the loop.

Later that day Ray Harford, the assistant manager of Blackburn Rovers, rang me and asked would I be interested in joining the club. They'd come in with an offer of £500,000, made up of cash plus Wayne Burnett, and it seemed that Shilton couldn't get me out of the door quickly enough. Not that I was about to turn down an offer like that.

Jack Walker's money had recently come into Rovers, who had just been promoted to the Premiership, and Kenny Dalglish was the manager. It is, I believe, known as a no-brainer so I jumped in my car and headed north to sign for a club awash with money and desperate for success. I was leaving the club I loved and the city I had made my home, but it was time to move on and take up a new challenge. What could possibly go wrong?

5

Fish Out of Water

The knowledge that one of the best players ever to grace the game wanted me to sign for him, and was prepared to pay half a million quid for the privilege, meant that, as far as I was concerned, the negotiations were going to be brief. Paula came with me to Blackburn while Arron stayed in Plymouth with his grandparents. We arrived around four and I was soon sitting in Kenny Dalglish's office. I had great respect for Kenny but I wasn't overwhelmed by him because my one and only hero was and remained Tommy Tynan and nobody was going to top that. Kenny asked me if I had an agent and I replied: 'Look, I trust you and trust you'll be fair with me.'

This was a massive move for me because in 1992 Blackburn were the Manchester City of their day. They were throwing money around, buying up the best players and sticking them on lucrative contracts. I couldn't have signed for a more ambitious club. Alan Shearer, whom I'd not seen since the Southampton training camp about eight years before, was the biggest name, but Paul Warhurst, Tim Flowers, Tim Sherwood and David Batty, to a man talented international players, had all recently joined.

We chatted for about an hour and Kenny seemed to be impressed that I didn't have an agent. He got up, went to have a chat with the club secretary and came back shortly after.

'Okay Andy. This is what I'd like to offer. I'll give you £800 per week plus £30,000 as a signing-on fee and £500 appearance money for three years, all index linked. How does that sound?' he asked.

It sounded fine to me.

I agreed on the spot and signed the contract as soon as it had been prepared. I had been thinking about something in the region of £700 plus £25,000 for signing-on so this was better than I'd hoped for – and he was chucking in the appearance money too. I was delighted. I was a Premier League player at last and I felt on top of the world. I knew, however, that I wasn't going to stroll into the starting eleven.

After I came out of the meeting a guy came up to me in the staff car park and told me he could sort out a new car out for me if I fancied trading in my Ford Fiesta XR2 for something 'a bit more upmarket'. It goes without saying every other player at the club was driving a top-of-the-range, flashy 4x4. That must have been how all new signings were greeted because there were estate agents handing me brochures, insurance guys punting policies and financial advisers trying to persuade me to invest my money with them. These guys knew that Premier League players offered rich pickings, although I gave them short shrift. It was a different world at Blackburn, a million miles from the council flat in Stonehouse. I wasn't sure what to make of it all and my head was spinning at the speed of events.

I still had the medical to get through and I was more than a little concerned because I was feeling a little twinge in my knee at that point. I had a cartilage operation not long before I left Argyle and I had started playing again far too soon, maybe as quickly as ten days after the op if my memory serves. It hadn't repaired correctly so I knew I would have to blag my way through the examination. An MRI scan would have revealed the extent of the damage, but they didn't think it was necessary, which was a relief because I knew it could have jeopardised the move. I made all the right moves with my knee and managed to cover the injury up enough to pass the tests. I then thanked the doc and left a happy and relieved man. I doubt I'm the first player to bluff his way through a medical and I won't be the last, although with all the technology that is now available it would be much more difficult in the modern game.

Paula and I went to a local hotel for the night to celebrate and we enjoyed a nice meal and had a couple of drinks, happy in the knowledge that I had gone from the third tier of English football to the Premier League. Next morning, Paula headed back to Plymouth for Arron while I went to Ewood Park to complete a few formalities. When that was done I posed for pictures for the local paper in a mechanical digger – don't ask – and then headed off to the training ground to begin life as a Blackburn Rovers player.

Paula was especially pleased with the move up north. She thought I would be able to leave both Plymouth and my problems behind me. If I went on behaving in the same irresponsible way my luck would soon run out. She saw it as a new chapter in our lives away from the temptation that my adopted home city held for me. My concern however was that Plymouth wasn't the problem. It was me who was the problem and I hadn't changed simply because I was at a new club. I was worried that my demons would resurface and I would have been naïve to have thought otherwise. In fact, I knew they would.

I was one of the first in at training the next day and I met Ray Harford, the assistant manager, and Tony Parkes from the coaching staff. Not many of the lads had arrived by that point, but there were a few familiar faces in the changing room, notably Shearer and Colin Hendry – only the captains of England and Scotland, then! That's probably when the magnitude of the move hit home for the first time. I had come from a club with ambition, but no money or infrastructure, to one that had ambition and probably more money than any other club in the country. For all my confidence and in-your-face attitude, I found the sight of those two quite intimidating and I couldn't help thinking, 'What the fuck am I doing here?' I was out of my comfort zone and out of my depth.

The rest of the players started to filter in and I don't think anyone really knew who I was. But they were friendly enough and they all came across and shook my hand. It wasn't until Nicky Marker, my old mate from Plymouth, came in that I settled down and had a bit of banter. The club had been signing all these superstars and I had arrived from little old Plymouth Argyle so it was no wonder I had something of an inferiority complex. I was aware of everything that was being said around me and was always switched on in that respect. I heard Mike Newell, Shearer's strike partner at the time, say to Jason Wilcox in hushed tones, 'I don't know who he is; I think he's come from Portsmouth.' I felt that Newell was looking at me as if to say, 'Who the fuck are you?' and I thought he was a touch arrogant and disrespectful. I later found out he was nothing of the sort and a really good lad, but it was an initial impression and one he was going to pay for in training.

An opportunity arose in my very first session.

Newell was about to go up for a ball and I saw my opportunity to correct him on one or two things. I steamed in to make the challenge and caught him with an elbow across the back of his head. He landed in a heap and stayed down for a few seconds so I went to help him back up.

'What the fuck are you doing?' he grimaced, rubbing his head. 'We both play for the same team in case you hadn't noticed.'

'I know. I'm sorry about that.'

As I heaved him to his feet, I added, 'And I come from Plymouth, not fucking Portsmouth.'

He looked confused, then it clicked that I'd overheard him in the changing room the previous day, so he said, 'fair play,' smiled and from that moment on we were mates. That was the first impression I made on any of the lads and to me it had been a good opportunity to leave my mark and show everyone that I was totally committed to the cause.

The session had gone well and shortly thereafter we left for a pre-season training camp in Ireland. We were due to play Drogheda, and the first thing that struck me was the reception that one of our lads, Kevin Moran, got wherever he went. This guy was a legend to the Irish people and he always had fifty people trailing in his wake. Dalglish and Shearer were also massively popular everywhere they went. It was a bit different from some of Argyle's pre-season games against Truro or Newquay!

It was funny being in the same team as Shearer. I remembered him from all those years ago as a teenager at Southampton and here he was, at the top of his game and already one of England's best strikers. Had I caught him up and progressed since our last meeting? I didn't think that was the case, but it made me realise that, for all my shortcomings, I must have been doing something right for the past four or five seasons.

Shearer was just returning from a cruciate operation and had been out for several months, so the first time I saw him play for the team was against Drogheda in our opening tour match. We were 2–0 down at the break but Shearer came off the bench at half-time and scored three times to turn the game on its head. He was one of the best in the business and for me that hat-trick summed him up. I just couldn't believe we were now teammates.

I made my debut in the next game, coming on for Moran in the last twenty minutes of our friendly with Shamrock Rovers. Within ten minutes I was aware that my knee wasn't right and it soon felt really sore. I played on and got through to the end even though I was in pain. Afterwards we all went on the lash. I was with Nicky Marker and Stuart Ripley, but there were no heavy drinkers in the squad and I quickly became aware that the likes of Shearer and players of his calibre kept a very low profile and would never be seen in clubs or going wild on the town. I think they had learned that, and much more besides, from Dalglish, a shrewd character who knew how to handle himself. Kenny behaved one way with the press and another with the lads. During interviews he was bland, could be very cutting and never gave anything away. Yet away from media scrutiny he would have a drink and a laugh with his coaching staff and morph into one of the lads when he was in the company of the players.

Dalglish needed to be canny with the media, as did all top-flight managers. The press, television and radio were becoming more and more interested in football, with the Premiership beginning to make football in this country far more glitzy. Players were fair game for scandal and exposés and there were plenty of people looking to make a quick buck at our expense. Things were changing. The money being bandied around made footballers big news; all of a sudden we were public property and of as much interest to the media as rock stars and actors. It happened almost overnight, but then again, all this was new to me. I was a small fish at the club, but if I started behaving the way I'd done at Plymouth, I'd soon be plastered all over the back pages, and maybe the front ones too. I would have to be careful about where and when I drank from now on.

Because of the squad we had, I knew I was way down the pecking order, but I'd known that before I signed. I just got my head down and worked hard in training. My reasoning was that if I did my best, my chance would eventually come along. The season began and I took my place in the reserves, but with Hendry, Moran, Henning Berg, Patrick Anderson and David May all ahead of me, it quickly became apparent I was hardly ever going to play. Looking back I'm not totally sure why they signed me because they had more than enough cover in the squad.

The pain in my knee was increasing every time I trained so I went to see the physio, had a scan and was told I had a tear on my cartilage, one that required surgery. It was no real surprise to me, but the fact that I would be sidelined for up to twelve weeks meant it was hardly a great start to life at Ewood Park. No doubt because of the stresses and strains of his job Kenny Dalglish couldn't pay a lot of attention to injured players and when I was out of the team it seemed to me that I was out of thoughts. He hadn't spoken too much to begin with, but, when I was sidelined, he pretty much blanked me and would do the same to anyone who was unavailable as far as I could tell. It wasn't personal, it was just the way he was and it reflected the huge pressure he was under to get results. I was already up against it at Blackburn, so this setback couldn't have come at a worse time. I could feel the depression starting to kick in.

6

King Kenny Rules

They talk about the Crazy Gang at Wimbledon and their legendary antics, but the squad at Blackburn – which had been assembled to win the title and to conquer Europe – were on a par. There were all kinds of characters at the club, and there was also a great camaraderie among the lads, and, whether I was playing or not, I enjoyed being around them. They were always at it, from trashing hotel rooms to pretty much anything you'd care to think of. David Batty, Paul Warhurst, Stuart Ripley and Jason Wilcox were great lads who loved the craic and, whenever there were high jinks, they would invariably be involved.

Tim Sherwood was a terrific lad who was also a great captain, someone who would do anything for the lads. Funny to be around and a dedicated professional he gave his all every time he trained and played. He was the sort of person I aspired to be, someone I looked up to. I remember that on one journey back from Aston Villa he wanted to play a game of chicken, and, after sorting out ten of us who were up for it, he put our names in a hat and drew them out one by one. The challenge was to tap the glass window at the back of the coach with a small toffee hammer, with each contestant having to tap it harder than the person who had gone before. If you failed to hit it hard enough your penalty was to put your finger out while it was hit with the hammer – not exactly a Christmas parlour game! Eventually, someone hit the glass too hard and the window exploded while we were doing seventy down the motorway. Dalglish shouted back to find out what was going on but we all acted dumb, saying it must have been a stone.

Graham Le Saux was a guy who some people didn't warm to because he was different from your stereotypical footballer. I travelled into training with him because we lived near to each other and I always got along well with him. So what that he read *The Observer* and went to antique fairs? If that's being different, we're all in big trouble. He didn't deserve either the negative press he got or the comments on the pitch from other players. He stood out from the crowd and he was an intelligent lad, but that was never a problem for me. I liked him and the fact that he was his own man. He was big enough to be himself and I respected him for that.

To me Alan Shearer was not a fantastic trainer and appeared to go through the motions, but during a game he was a different animal altogether. We often had practice matches between the first team and the reserves and I can honestly say he never had anything that bothered me in those games. Kevin Gallagher gave me problems with his pace and trickery, but Shearer didn't and I always wondered how he could turn in brilliant performances on such a consistent basis after seeming to coast through the week. He was one of a select band.

People have called me a hard man throughout my career but I don't know which criteria people use to determine 'hardness'. I have never thought of myself in that way. I can handle myself, but David Batty took that side of the game to a different level. I remember one occasion when we were away to Southampton and Batty went up for a header with Francis Benali, whose elbow split the side of David's head open. There was blood pouring down his face and our bench shouted for him to come off, or at least to go down so that he could receive treatment and stem the blood. David ignored them and carried on as if nothing had happened. I saw him later and said, 'Your head was pissing out with blood. Why didn't you fucking stop?'

He just smiled: 'I wasn't fucking touching it because, if I had, he might think that he'd done me. I just carried on so the fucker didn't have the satisfaction.'

The thing with Batty was that nobody ever gave him credit for being a great player, apart that is from the lads who trained and played alongside him. If you had a small-sided game or a keep-ball session, you wanted Batty on your team because he never gave the ball away. However, because he had a reputation for being hard, most people had him tagged as little more than a thug. I rate him in a similar bracket to Paul Scholes, although without the same goal-scoring ratio.

Despite Jack Walker's money, I was surprised by the state of Rovers' training facilities and there was more than a hint that the club was running before it could walk. We had arguably the best manager in the country, and some of the best players in the world, yet we were training on council-owned pitches at Pleasington, pitches that weren't much better than a cow patch. It was ludicrous that they were risking multi-million pound footballers on surfaces like that. It was like training thoroughbred horses on cobbled streets and, for all Blackburn's ambition, Argyle's training facilities were far superior. New facilities were being built at Brockhole but in the meantime a number of the lads picked up injuries as a result of the conditions. Too many strains occurred on those pitches for it to be a coincidence, as well as numerous cuts and grazes. But I couldn't blame the injury I was sidelined with on the state of Pleasington.

I had been out for three months and the depression was as bad as any I had suffered. I was missing Plymouth and felt my career at Blackburn was going nowhere, largely as a result of my own eager-ness to start playing again. I was paying a hefty price and watching the lads from the stands as they made a real bid for the title. That didn't make life any easier, even though I knew it would have taken an injury crisis that an episode of *Casualty* would have been proud of for me to have got a first-team place.

Away from football, I had generally behaved myself for the first four or five months, keeping a fairly low profile. But all that was about to change at the Christmas party Tim Sherwood had organ-ised at a place called the French Bistro in Preston. Our families and friends were invited and there were guests from all over the coun-try, including quite a few up from London. Towards the early hours and with a skinful of beer inside me, I went to the toilet for a leak. Depression and beer aren't a great mix and because I was unsteady on my feet, I wasn't aiming straight at the urinal. Some piss must have sprayed off onto the guy next to me, who said something. I told him to push off. He finished peeing, turned away, and walked out, or so I thought. As I turned around, he punched me in the face, taking me completely by surprise. There is nothing like a right hook to sober you up and within seconds I was laying into him. I can't recall what happened next, because I blacked out as I had done a couple of times before when the madness began. He ended up with a big gouge in his head and in an almighty mess on the floor. It was horrible, and not something I'm proud of, but there it is. As was often the case during one of my drink-fuelled mad turns it felt like someone else had done it rather than me. One of the lads took the guy to hospital, where I believe he stayed for a few days. It turned out that he was a mate of Tim Sherwood's, but, because he had started it, Tim accepted it had been a situation of his own making. The guy I laid out decided not to take things any further. My luck, if that's what you want to call it, was still intact. Inevitably, the club got wind of it the following day and it no doubt further hindered my chances of making it at Blackburn. Whether Dalglish knew of my previous record of violence in Plymouth, I'm not sure, but he knew now and it was probably another nail in my coffin as far as he was concerned.

No matter how many times I swore I'd stop, there was something deep inside me, driving me towards trouble. I went out drinking on my own at weekends and those sessions invariably ended with me fighting with strangers after I'd gone into what I called my 'dead zone'. The only good thing, if you can call it that, was that something in my consciousness stopped me from going too far. Paula always knew when something had happened because I would come home with cuts, grazes and scraped knuckles. She always gave me a lecture, but, in an odd way, she became used to it and in those days seemed to accept it.

At the club, I was training on my own. My knee still didn't feel right and, as a result, I began taking anti-inflammatory tablets for the first time. I was two weeks beyond the point that had been scheduled for the resumption of full training and I still felt a way off being declared fit to play. I began taking Ibuprofen pills in a bid to speed up the process and the following day my knee felt great. Those magic little pink tablets were about to become a lifelong friend and thanks to their ability to ease the pain, I started training again. Then, just a couple of days after I returned, the Pleasington pitches added me to their long list of victims. I took a tumble on an uneven part of the ground and split my kneecap open. I needed six stitches in a nasty gash, which sidelined me for another ten days. I don't know what the coaching staff made of me but I am sure it would have been along the lines of 'What the fuck have we signed here? This guy is a fucking liability.'

The wound healed but on my first day back at Pleasington I went over on my knee again, which left me with an even deeper gash than before. As a result I had to have surgery to repair and properly clean the cut, which meant another month out. I was shattered. I had been out for the best part of five months. Signing for Blackburn, I felt, had been jinxed from the start. It wasn't until the New Year that I managed to get fully fit and have a good run of games in the reserves. Finally, perhaps, I was beginning to make the right impression on Dalglish and the backroom staff. I felt strong and was free from pain for the first time in a long while. Even better, my form led to a couple of appearances on the bench for the first team and then, at last, I made my competitive debut.

We were up against Wimbledon at Ewood Park and five minutes into the game Kevin Moran pulled up with a hamstring injury. I went to warm up and Dalglish told me I was to slot in alongside Colin Hendry in the back four. It was the chance I had been waiting for and, if ever a game was suited to my style of play, this was it. Wimbledon had John Fashanu and Dean Holdsworth up front and I couldn't get on quick enough. They were a handful and could be intimidating, but I wasn't worried. Fashanu had a peculiar habit of saying that a particular area at set-pieces was 'Fashanu's space,' which was music to my ears. I had five months of frustration that I needed to get out of my system so, the first chance I got, I smashed into him – fairly – and left him in a heap on the deck. Ray Harford later told me that Dalglish winced when he saw me make the challenge, wondering if I knew who I was taking on. But nothing came back from Fash and we went on to win 3–0, with me being voted sponsor's man of the match. Things had gone better than I had dared to hope. Maybe, at long last, I had convinced Dalglish that he had been right to take a punt on me. Just as importantly I felt I had proved myself to the other lads. For the first time, I felt part of the team.

'Well done. You looked like you enjoyed yourself out there,' Dalglish grinned, his first words to me in five months. Ray meanwhile put his arm around my neck and uttered just one word: 'awesome'. Later he told me that he was the one who had stuck his neck out by recommending me and that he saw a lot of Kevin Moran's qualities in me, which was quite a compliment for a 22-year-old.

I kept my place for the next game – in the FA Cup at home to Charlton Athletic – which we were expected to win comfortably. I had another good game and was up against Carl Leaburn, a big, strong brute of a lad, but we lost 2–1. Watching the highlights on *Match of the Day*, I took an instant dislike to Alan Hansen, who happened to be a big mate of Dalglish's. In his analysis, he suggested that our squad didn't have enough strength in depth and that with Moran injured there were deficiencies that needed to be addressed, all of which I took to be a personal dig at me. I thought Hansen was out of order because I had given my all and neither goal was a result of errors I had made. Perhaps however Dalglish leant towards his old pal's assessment because, for the next match, David May was fit again and I was dropped to the bench.

I travelled everywhere with the squad but as the injuries cleared up my chances of playing were limited. Although we were five points behind Manchester United in the title race, there was still everything to play for with two games left and who knew what might happen if results went our way? We were away to Coventry City, a game that was live on *Sky Sports*. Ray Harford told me on the Thursday that I would be starting the game, but as I had been told before by Ray that I was in, only for Dalglish to change his mind an hour before kickoff and leave me out, I didn't get over excited. It was a massive game for us and so I was relieved when the team was read out and my name was included.

It would have been better if I had stayed on the bench.

Like any player, I had my strengths and weaknesses: put me up against a big, tough, uncompromising striker and I was in my element; small, speedy wingers were not, however, my forte and Coventry City's Zimbabwean forward Peter Ndlovu, who was in the form of his career, gave me a torrid afternoon. With the game tied at 1–1 we became more and more desperate as we looked for the winner that would keep our title hopes alive. We threw everyone forward, leaving me exposed time and time again, which was a risk that backfired as Ndlovu tore me to pieces during a couple of counter-attacks. With fifteen minutes to go Dalglish had seen enough. He took me off and put Nicky Marker on. I was gutted because I had worked incredibly hard in training to get fit and had not let the team down when called upon. I had managed to get ahead of Nicky in the pecking order but had failed this particular audition, handing him the opportunity to shine. I was disconsolate and as I trudged off the pitch I felt it might be my last chance in the first team. I was right; I never played for Blackburn Rovers again. We lost the Coventry game by two goals to one, Manchester United won the title and I realised it was inevitable that I would be moving on again soon. You don't let Kenny Dalglish down and live to tell the tale.

The summer passed without incident and despite me being even further out in the cold, I wasn't going to sulk. I came back for pre-season feeling sharp and in good nick physically. After a week of building up our fitness, we headed off to play Jersey in a pre-season friendly that Jack Walker had arranged. It was a massive game for the islanders and having players of the calibre of Shearer and Flowers around was like having movie stars in town. We flew from Manchester and then got on the team coach to travel to the hotel, but, before we reached our destination, Tim Sherwood gave each player £1,500. Don't ask me where he got it from; perhaps it was a player's pool or money that had come in from sponsors. Whatever the source I wasn't complaining.

I liked Jersey and enjoyed the friendly we played against them and the meal afterwards. Later, we went out to a nightclub in St Hellier, where we were treated like celebrities and given a magnum of champagne each, all of which made me realise how far I'd come since my days with Plymouth. Not that long ago I had been in a spit-and-sawdust pub at the fish quay drinking scrumpy with bits of wood in the bottom. Now I was supping champagne in a swanky club. Obviously, I wished I was playing a bigger part in the team, but I was determined to enjoy the moment to the full. We didn't spend a penny and were constantly having our glasses refilled. It was fascinating to be part of but I still felt like an outsider, as though I was watching from a distance. It reinforced my feeling that I didn't belong amongst these famous international footballers.

To add to the surrealism, Dalglish's mate, golfer Ian Woosnam, had been invited along to the do and, somehow, I ended up arm wrestling him at £50 a pop. I won with ease and had taken £250 off him without breaking sweat. He was getting more and more wound up because he fancied himself the strong man and he had these little Popeye forearms that must have given him a real advantage in most situations. But not that night. He asked to swap to left arms, but I still beat him. He then wanted to up the stakes, but Kenny stepped in and said to Woosie that he'd had enough for one evening and to stick to the golf.

Sky Sports and the Premiership may have taken the game to a different level but the bottom line was that, despite the champagne lifestyle, fast cars and big pay packets, I was a working-class lad who had been brought up in a rough neighbourhood. There is a very true saying: you can take the boy from the slum but not the slum from the boy. That was so true of me at Blackburn. I missed the rawness and in-your-face reality of Plymouth.

The good thing was that I was in great shape going into the new season and was nearing my peak in the reserves, a handy team that included the likes of Shay Given and Nicky Marker. However, despite our undoubted ability we had our ass kicked by a bunch of kids at Old Trafford. We had a strong eleven out that day, with me, Paul Warhurst, Nicky Marker, Tim Sherwood and Colin Hendry up against a Man United second string made up of youngsters and academy lads. Not that it made much difference. They beat us 4–0 and the lads we faced that day – David Beckham, Paul Scholes, Nicky Butt, Ryan Giggs, Terry Cooke, Ben Thornley and the Neville brothers – would form the backbone of the United team that would dominate English football for the next ten years. They were phenomenal. We weren't able to get the ball off them, and, despite myself, I couldn't help but admire their accurate passing and sublime technique. It was the only time in my career that I faced Beckham, but he and his team-mates were awesome.

While I languished in the reserves it was perhaps inevitable that other teams would see an opportunity to sign me. There were rumours that Celtic were interested and, being a proud Scot, it goes without saying I would have snapped off their hands for a move to Parkhead, even if I had more of an affinity with Rangers. I believe they came to watch me a few times, but I don't think they got much encouragement from Blackburn. It had been all over the papers in Blackburn and Plymouth that they were closely following my progress, but I never had the chance to speak to them. They eventually signed a guy called John Hughes from Hibs and the opportunity was gone. Maybe they had asked around and been told, 'Don't touch him with a bargepole; he's nothing but trouble.' It's a shame because I would have loved the chance to play for a club like Celtic, and I think I would have gone down well with the Parkhead faithful, but it wasn't to be.

I had a bit of a fright a few months into the new campaign. During training one of the girls from the office informed me that my wife was in a bit of a state and needed me to come home right away. I raced to my car and got to the house in no time at all. I wondered what the hell had happened, panicking in case it was something I had done. Because of the occasional blackouts I suffered when I was drunk, I was always afraid that something was going to come back to haunt me. I pulled into the drive of the converted barn we were living in and ran inside. Paula was standing on a table, white as a sheet, looking shaken and tearful.

'There's a mouse in here,' she screamed. A wave of relief spread over me. Arron was in his high chair, looking suitably bemused.

'Take me to a hotel,' she said. 'I can't stay here while that thing is loose.' I helped her down, got Arron and put them both in the car. One scrawny mouse! Unbelievable. I couldn't help but smile, half relieved it hadn't been anything more serious. I took her to the hotel and called out pest control.

One lad I became good mates with was new signing Chris Sutton, who would go on to become one half of the famous SAS – Sutton and Shearer – partnership. Sutty, a very intelligent lad, had signed from Norwich for £5.5 million and I immediately hit it off with him, which was strange because we were two completely different characters. He was carefree and easy-going whereas, to say the least, I wasn't. We travelled into training together and our wives also got on well and we all enjoyed each other's company. Paradoxically, despite

Chris's relaxed attitude to life in general, he was one of the world's great worriers when it came to football. In the dressing room before a game he would say things like, 'I'm not sure about this lot. I've never scored against them before,' or he would be anxious about the defender he would be up against in case he was the bullying type. Then, come kickoff, he underwent yet another personality change, turning into the man who wasn't worried about anything or anyone. He got right into opponents' faces and he wouldn't back down, something I could relate to. I never sussed out if he was putting on a show in the car, putting on a show in the dressing room or putting on a show when he took to the pitch because surely no one could undergo such profound personality changes in such a short space of time. Whatever the explanation it certainly didn't affect his performances. He was terrific at holding up the ball, great at bringing others into the play and most important of all he scored goals. I was chuffed that things went so well for him. He was the perfect foil for Shearer and with wingers Wilcox and Ripley supplying the ammunition we had a formidable attack that I enjoyed watching, albeit from the stands!

Any lingering hopes I had of somehow getting back into the side were swept away on a UEFA Cup trip to Trelleborgs of Sweden. They had a big striker who was giving our back four a right battering, and, after sixty-five minutes, one of our central defenders came off injured. It was the perfect opportunity for me to come off the bench and prove that I still had a part to play at the club – horses for courses and all that – but Dalglish brought on Ian Pearce instead. It was the final snub and I knew that my time with Rovers was up. I later asked Ray Harford why I hadn't been brought on and he told me that after the vital game against Coventry at the end of the previous season Dalglish had lost faith in me. It wasn't what I wanted to hear, but it was maybe what I needed to hear. The writing was on the wall in letters ten feet high. I had to find another club and the sooner the better.

A few days later I was told that former Liverpool and England midfielder Steve McMahon, now manager at Swindon, wanted to take me on loan. I set off down the motorway and had got as far as Charnock Richard when I got another call on my mobile, this time from Billy Bingham, who was working as a sort of middle man for Blackpool chairman Owen Oyston and his manager Sam Allardyce.

He asked if I would be interested in signing for the Seasiders. They had made a bid of £250,000 and it had had been accepted by Rovers. I turned my car around and headed back up the M6.

Dalglish called me before I met up with Blackpool. He said: 'Look, a bid has come in that we're happy with, but you don't have to go. I'm happy with the way you train and play so there's no pressure on you. Go and see what they've got to say, but, if you're not sure, and you decide you want to stay with us, that's fine with me.

The club rang McMahon at Swindon and told him I wouldn't be coming after all. In the meantime I was eager to hear what third division Blackpool had to say and so I met Oyston, Bingham and chief executive Gill Bridge at a hotel near Preston. They weren't football people – at least not my type – and after an hour of talks with them I was having second thoughts about the move. Maybe I would stay at Ewood Park after all.

7

Tangerine Dream

It's funny how first impressions stay with you. My initial impression of Billy Bingham was that he was trying to rip me off and get me on the cheap.

'What are you looking for?' he asked. That pissed me off straight-away. I can't be bothered negotiating or engaging in small talk and he would have been well aware of what I was on at Blackburn so we didn't make the best of starts.

'I'm looking for a pay-cut, no appearance money and no signing-on fee,' I replied, in a suitably sarcastic tone.

Bridge, Oyston and Bingham smiled but I didn't. I wanted them to come to me with an offer, not piss about trying to save £100 here or there. Big Sam wasn't there at first – he was away watching a youth-cup match – but he eventually arrived and joined in the nego-tiations. I was glad he was there. He was a big, imposing man with a strong handshake and he just wanted to talk football, which was a relief because I was losing patience. Bingham offered me £250 a week plus a signing-on fee that would make up the shortfall in the wage I'd been on and the wage I'd be on. I told him and Gill Bridge, the chairman's PA, that I would go away and think about it.

I spoke with Paula about the proposed move and she was her usual, relaxed self saying we should wait and see what Blackburn had to say. I went into training and saw Ray Harford before the session. I valued Ray's opinion and wanted to hear his view, particularly as he'd been the one who had believed in me and helped me move to Rovers.

'Do what's right for you and your family,' he said. Then Kenny arrived and I was told to go and see him in his office. Billy Bingham had been on the phone.

'There's no pressure on you to leave, Andy. Like I said, I'm happy if you want to stay here and fight for a place in the squad if that's what you want to do, but just do what you feel is right.'

I finished training with the reserves, had lunch and went home. Bingham called me in mid-afternoon and said: 'Look, we've changed our wage structure and you're the reason we've done it. You'd better sign for us now.'

That they had gone to such lengths impressed me and I drove to Blackpool for another chat with Sam. Even though this was his first managerial position he had a real aura about him. I liked him and wanted to play for him. He was honest, friendly and open and I relished what he had to say. He began to tell me about the club's plans, the proposed new stadium and the way forward. He added there were some really nice places to live within a short drive, but I had heard enough.

'Stop. You don't have to sell the club to me. The fact that you want me to sign is enough for me. I don't need to think about whether or not my wife will settle in the area because I'm here to play football.'

In spite of that, he told me to go away and have a think, so I did. I spoke with my dad and Paula and some of the lads at Blackburn, as well as Ray Harford, who thought it would be a great move because I would be playing regularly again and going to a club with ambition. My mind made up, I called Sam and told him I was going to sign.

I was offered £700 and a £21,000 signing-on fee, split into three payments. I thought that was fair and so I signed the contract. The good thing was that because I hadn't asked to leave Blackburn I would still be paid the two signing-on fees I would have got if I'd stayed at Ewood Park. All in all I would receive the best part of £60,000 as a sweetener. The move ticked a lot of boxes for me. I would also be near the sea again, which I had missed.

Sam was delighted. He told me he wanted me to play in front of the back four because I had played seventy-odd games for Plymouth in midfield and he had a role in mind for me. I was just happy that I was back in the first-team picture. I had a good feeling about the move and was looking forward to putting my heart and soul into the club and seeing where it took me.

In hindsight, Blackburn was a demoralising experience, a backward step in my career. I learned a lot about the game from great players and good coaches at Ewood Park, something I would take with me for the rest of my career. But overall it was a negative experience. I had gone from being player of the year and a crowd idol at Plymouth to a place where I wasn't rated that highly. I am a proud man and my pride had been hurt, simply because I hadn't been able to prove myself. Blackburn had been a dark period so I was glad to be leaving for pastures new. I looked forward to a new challenge.

As a father and a husband my life should have been more settled than it had ever been. It didn't pan out that way. In fact, my time at Bloomfield Road was set to eclipse everything I had done previously, either on or off the pitch. The word explosive comes to mind when I think of my escapades up there.

With all the paperwork in order and a medical passed without having to cover up any old injuries, I arrived for training early to find a rundown building with changing rooms, a gym and a huge team bath. Everything looked dilapidated and old school. I felt at home straightaway! It was a million miles from Blackburn's new state-of-the-art training facility at Brockhole and there was none of the one-to-one pampering that was beginning to creep into top-level football with masseurs, dieticians and the like.

I loved being back among a team of lads who had everything to prove and nothing to lose. It was liberating and a big part of the reason there was such a great camaraderie. Sam was trying to build something at Blackpool and he had a vision of where the club should be and how it should get there. There were a number of other new faces and the plan was to add a few more to the squad. I couldn't wait to get started and, as the club's record signing, I felt I owed Sam and the fans. My only guarantee was total commitment each time I pulled on that tangerine shirt.

At last, the day of my first game arrived and it couldn't have gone much better because I managed to get on the score-sheet in a 3–1 win over Bournemouth. It was the perfect start and the supporters seemed to take to me. I was playing as a holding midfielder, which meant I could get forward more often. It was a tactical innovation that became something of trademark for Sam as he moved up through the managerial ranks. I think you could label it as the 'Ivan Campo' role.

I received a bottle of champagne after being voted man of the match and I was well chuffed. There was, however, a sting in the tail. I was told that everyone making their debut was voted man of the match, no matter how crap they had been! It was Billy Bingham's idea, apparently. Next up we were away to Neil Warnock's Huddersfield Town and we drew 1–1. After the game Warnock told me he would have loved to have signed me had he known I was available for transfer. That was nice to hear. No matter who you are, comments like that are good for your ego.

I couldn't have been happier with the start I had made at Bloomfield Road and it should have been a sign of things to come. I had a new club, a nice contract, a great manager, adoring fans and the opportunity to put my troubles behind me. But yet again I was incapable of keeping my nose clean.

I was invited to attend a fan forum with Sam, skipper Phil Brown and teammate Micky Mellon. We stayed over in a hotel because we were training the next day and after the question-and-answer session a few of us went into town for a beer. Micky and I eventually went back to the hotel and continued to drink into the early hours. We started a debate as to which part of Scotland true Scotsmen were from, pathetic I know, but it went on and on.

Micky was from Glasgow and therefore a Lowlander whereas I was, of course, a Highlander from Kinlochbervie. At first it was light-hearted and good fun, but at some point I began to lose the argument and snapped. Within seconds Micky was left in a right mess on the floor. As usual, I had no recollection of what happened in those few explosive seconds, only the events leading up to it. I went to my room to sleep it off and woke up with 'The Four Hideous Horsemen' as they are known: terror, fear, bewilderment and regret. I still couldn't see that, though I didn't get into trouble every time I drank, every time I had got into trouble, I had drunk. The penny wouldn't drop, perhaps because I didn't want it to. Now I had to face big Sam Allardyce.

I got into the training ground at nine the next morning and waited for the manager. Bobby Saxton, the first-team coach, was already in and I explained to him what had happened. He phoned Sam, who was in his car. I trained as usual after being told by Phil Brown that Sam 'would deal with it later'. Micky didn't show for training and in fact wouldn't appear for another few days. I showered and then went and knocked on Sam's door. Sam was there with Bobby Saxton. I was told to sit down.

'Right, what happened?' Sam sighed. 'This is all I fucking need.'

Throughout my career I had caused headaches for numerous managers but I had always taken the view that it was my problem and mine alone. That of course was a blinkered and selfish attitude. Managers live or die by the signings they make and the guys they choose to put on the park. A player's behaviour isn't just his concern; it is a concern for the man who sits in the manager's office. Sam would now need to explain to the chairman why he had signed me and would probably get a bollocking for not doing his homework properly. It wasn't fair on Sam, especially when I had only been at the club for a fortnight. But he did his best for me, telling me he would sort it out. Sam also said he would speak with Micky Mellon to see if he could straighten things out with him.

Word got around the dressing room and a few of the lads asked me what had happened. I told them that I honestly didn't know why I'd done what I'd done. I left a voice message on Micky's phone but I didn't hear back from him until the following evening, when he called me at home. I didn't know what to say and was both embarrassed and ashamed.

'I think things deteriorated when I mentioned they put stockings on sheep up your end before shagging them,' said Micky, making light of it. 'That's what pushed you over the edge.' He was making a joke of it, which was a relief, and the next day at training we sat down with Sam and shook hands. We put it down to drink, an excuse I had made on far too many occasions already. I told Sam it wouldn't happen again, although I was careful not to say that I wouldn't drink again.

I was gambling with my career every time I drank. Each time I started, I had a roulette wheel in front of me but instead of numbers, it had words: police, hospital, cells, my house, someone else's house, dead. I was in a downward spiral that I had no control over. In the pub I would meet fans, drink with them and end up at a party. All that was important was that I had someone to drink with. I couldn't see that there was only one possible ending. My final hangover would be in the mortuary.

8

Just One Notch Below Attempted Murder

Blackpool is a funny town. In the summer it's packed with day trippers plus countless hen and stag parties and then the illuminations kick in during the autumn, bringing the punters flocking back. After that, it pretty much shuts down and it's the bleakest place on earth, a wind-and-rain-battered ghost town with a few pubs staying open and not much else. Despite that, I loved the club and I loved the town. After a few months in charge of Blackpool, Ian Holloway remarked that he and the town had one thing in common: they both looked better with the lights off. I knew where he was coming from.

I managed to stay out of trouble for the rest of the season, and I did well on the pitch, but we fizzled out somewhat and I finished my first campaign with the Seasiders in mid-table. Sam continued to mould the squad in his own image, adding a couple more signings during the summer. Phil Brown was coming towards the end of his playing career and I felt proud when I was handed the captain's armband on the eve of the 1995/96 season. It was my reward for training and playing hard and being true to my word. It was also no doubt because of the great rapport I had with the fans.

I'm not sure why supporters took to me the way they did. I like to think it's because they see me as one of their own, an ordinary, working-class bloke who can play football. Just as they had done at Plymouth, the Blackpool fans loved it when I went in with a full-blooded challenge. They knew there were no half-measures and there was probably an element of notoriety due to my off-field problems.

Whatever it was, it was appreciated and it only made me try even harder.

We were determined to give it a really good go in 95/96 because we felt we could get ourselves into the second division with the team we had. There was hunger and plenty of experience in the side and although Sam was just starting out on his management career, we all loved him and were eager to repay the faith he had shown in us. I felt I was at the peak of my powers: we had a terrific pre-season and I was now wearing the skipper's armband. If ever there was an opportunity to move my life in another direction, this was it. I'd had a quiet summer with my family, got fit and really looked after myself. Things couldn't have been going any better, but how did I reward myself? That's right, by having a few days on the lash back home in Plymouth.

We had been given a couple of days off so I phoned some mates in Plymouth to see if they fancied a night out over the August bank-holiday weekend on the eve of the new season. Like Dad always said, I just didn't learn my lessons. I travelled south and met up with two of the mates I'd done my apprenticeship with at Argyle: Darren Tallon and Owen Pickard. We headed off to Union Street for a night out. It was good to be home again and although I had been back a couple of times before, it would be my first real bender for three months.

We went into the Phoenix, a pub about a mile from where I had been brought up. It was a real spit-and-sawdust place and I always think of it as the bar Hans Solo goes into during the first *Star Wars* movie, full of freaky-looking people, most of them with broken noses. The question I should have been asking myself was, 'Why do I need to go to a place like this?' It wasn't that long since I had been drinking champagne with Alan Shearer and Kenny Dalglish, so what the fuck could I gain by visiting one of my old haunts? There were some nice wine bars in Plymouth, some just two minutes down the road, yet here I was, like a pig in shit. More to the point, why did I need to drag two of my oldest mates in there with me? Especially when they were doing everything they could to get me to go somewhere else. Maybe I was trying to prove that I wasn't a Billy Big Time and that I hadn't changed since my days in the Stonehouse council flat.

If there was a ruck, there was a good chance nobody would ever know about it because it would more than likely get swept under the carpet. Who would care if it kicked off in the Phoenix? It happened all the time in there. I knew all that, yet here we were. Bare floor-boards, no curtains and air of malice. We couldn't have been in there more than five minutes when six of the regulars recognised me. I was in the local papers a lot, being a former Argyle lad, and I had a few quid. I guess I cut a pretty recognisable figure, so it wasn't a shock that people knew who I was. Three of the six just wanted the craic, but the other three gave me the distinct impression that they were intent on winding me up. The digs came thick and fast.

'Why the fuck are you in here? Why are you drinking with us lot? Fucking big time aren't you mate? Shouldn't you be somewhere else? I could have been better than you. You're fucking shit, mate.'

The logical choice was to let it go and Owen recognised as much, 'Why don't we just fuck off out of here?' he asked.

In normal circumstances that wasn't an option. However, I ignored them and walked away. Maybe I was making progress after all.

'Let's finish our drinks first,' I said. We walked over to the DJ and started chatting among ourselves, minding our own business. But the same prick who'd been giving out before came over again, only this time he'd brought his two mates with him for company. It was obvious what was coming next. He started prodding me in the chest. Finally, he got the response he wanted. I exploded.

I had the worst blackout of my life and I don't recall much else. Owen and Darren held back the other three as I went at it with my three tormentors. After ninety seconds of carnage it was all over. I looked like the Tasmanian Devil but they were even worse. One had a broken nose and a smashed jaw, another had half his eyebrow missing while the third was off in the toilet looking the worse for wear. I can't explain why I blacked out – I never could – I just suddenly developed what I can only describe as superhuman strength. Darren and Owen later told me that no one could have stopped me. I had been like a wild animal.

I am sure that 99.9 per cent of all footballers would never have gone to a place like that because the end result is so predictable. And even if they had gone into a dive like the Phoenix most would have turned tail at the first hint of trouble. We left the pub and as we were walking down the road a police car pulled up. The officer knew who I was and he informed me that I fitted the description of someone who was wanted for a violent incident in the Phoenix. He said he wasn't going to arrest me, but that he'd give me a lift to the station where we would see how things developed. I got in the car with Darren – Owen having left by that point – and went along to the station. After being questioned, I was charged with a Section 18 on one of the lads, which in layman's terms is malicious wounding with intent and just one notch below attempted murder. I was also charged with actual bodily harm on one of the other lads and assault and battery in respect of the third. Finally, they were throwing the book at me and this time I couldn't see a way out.

While the other local lads who were present admitted their three mates had been the agitators, they all agreed that I had gone too far. I was released on bail and I travelled back to Blackpool to face the music yet again. I felt it hadn't been entirely of my making, which was a first, but I had made a rod for my own back because who would now believe that I hadn't started it? I spoke to Sam at length and although he backed me publicly, I felt he didn't fully believe me and he no doubt thought I would let him down again. I told him I was going to fight the charges because I had been provoked and that I wasn't going to lie down and accept a guilty plea. What I had done was wrong, but I should have been allowed to drink wherever I wanted. The three lads, pissed or not, had grabbed the tiger's tail.

Owen Oyston was informed and he instructed the same lawyers who were working on a case he was involved in to defend me, with the understanding that I would pay the legal fees at a later date. It turned out I had been granted the services of Anthony Scrivener QC, no less, perhaps the best barrister in the country and a man who, ten years later, would attempt to defend Saddam Hussein on charges of war crimes. He was a friend of Owen's, and he had a great legal team alongside him, but the most important factor was that the prosecution's main witness was my best mate Darren Tallon. He had seen exactly what happened and would be completely truthful in court. If he was their main man, I knew I had a decent chance of walking free.

On the pitch, I was innocent until proven guilty and we were having a cracking season. I refused to let a potential jail term affect my performances. Sam asked me if I was all right to play and it was more a case of 'try and stop me'. We were playing some good football and were among the promotion places right from the off.

By the time my case got into court, Mr Scrivener had met with Sam and me. He explained that if I was found guilty, I would go to prison for a minimum of four years and probably serve at least two-and-a-half years of that sentence. Sam nearly fell off his chair when he heard that, because while this was all too real for me, he had only just realised how serious the situation was. I had to go back to Plymouth for the trial, which under normal circumstances could have been a problem as I might have been tempted out for a piss-up. However, as part of my bail conditions, I was banned from entering any licensed premises in the city. My barrister said that he had never come across a condition like that before, but it was a wise clause for the judge to have to put in and one that was greatly to my benefit.

The trial in Plymouth Crown Court lasted for a week and as each day passed I grew more and more confident. Things just seemed to go my way from day one. The jury went out to examine the scene of the fight and the one thing that really stood out during their visit to the Phoenix was the foot rail around the bar. It was suggested by my brief that one of the lads' injuries could have been caused by falling on to the rail. That could well have been the case, I had no idea, but it planted a seed of doubt in the jury's mind and when that was added to the rest of the evidence I felt I had a real chance of being acquitted. And that is exactly how it turned out. When the verdicts were read out it was a resounding 'not guilty' on all charges. I felt a massive weight lift off my shoulders.

The press were out in force but I didn't say a word. I was just relieved that I could continue my playing career and that I wouldn't be going to HMP Dartmoor. I celebrated with my family in the only way I knew how. The definition of insanity, I'm led to believe, is doing the same thing over and over again and expecting a different result. Bearing that in mind, you can predict what happened next.

I went out for a drink with my dad and brothers, who all made me swear that I would never put myself in such a predicament again. We carried on celebrating and by one in the morning it was just Ian and me left drinking. Needless to say I was pissed and on the brink of doing something I would live to regret. I was always pushing my luck, being fully aware of what might happen but enjoying the risk nevertheless. We got into a cab but jumped out at a kebab shop and, as ever at chucking-out time in such establishments up and down the land, there were several other pissed-up lads waiting for their order. Imagine taking a lighted match into a gunpowder factory; an explosion is always imminent. That's how it was in the kebab shop. I'd been in there less than five minutes before the 'other' Andy Morrison forgot that it was just a few hours since I'd been spared a four-year prison term. A wrong look, a few words exchanged. Who knows? I don't, but the next thing I knew I'd decked some guy. The police arrived within minutes and arrested me.

There wouldn't be a not-guilty verdict this time. I'd get what I'd managed to avoid for so long, a prison sentence. Yet, despite there being no defence for what I'd done, for reasons unknown to me, the lad I had punched didn't want to press charges. That was the end of it as far as the police were concerned and I was on my way. By this point you're no doubt thinking that if I fell in a barrel of shit I'd come out smelling of roses and, in some ways, you'd be right.

It was a ludicrous situation to be in because I had endured six months of hell wondering whether I was going to jail or not and yet here I was risking everything because I couldn't control my drinking. This was not a week, or a month or a year later, but the very day on which I had been cleared of a serious assault charge. In a parallel universe, the guy presses charges and I go to jail. In that same parallel universe the club sacks me and nobody in football wants any more to do with me. I got what I'd been asking for and become a pariah, washed up at the age of twenty-five. That's what I deserved, yet somehow I got away with it again.

The problem was that I never knew where the next marathon session would lead me, though there was always a chance it would end with some kind of violent episode. I didn't always end up in trouble and sometimes I could be happy and go home having had a great night out. People will come to the conclusion that I was insane and the truth is, with drink inside me, I was. Anything could happen when that chamber was spinning, but sooner or later it would spin to the one with the bullet and that would be an end on it. Instead,

I woke up the next day, had a laugh with Ian and headed back to Blackpool, freedom and career miraculously intact.

Some people may be wondering what Paula, my dear wife, thought of my many scrapes with the law. The answer is that I tried to shield her from the possible implications of me being found guilty. I knew what it meant and what the damage being sent to prison would inflict on our lives, but I managed to play it down so that she never got too worried. She knew the situation and the events that had surrounded the case and because of that, I don't think she ever felt I was in danger of being sent to prison.

If I had been found guilty, I would have been sent to jail for three or four years – maybe more – so I don't know where that would have left us as a family. We could have lost our house and my career would have been as good as over. Potentially, it was catastrophic. Who knows what kind of knock-on effect that would have had. Instead, we stayed positive throughout the trial, either through a belief that I wasn't guilty or just wishful thinking.

It wasn't until the case was over and we had the debrief with the defence team that Paula realised how much shit I'd been in. She was well aware of how trouble used to find me, and she saw for herself on numerous occasions the kind of pricks who sought me out, so she never doubted my side of the story. She never gave me ultimatums and just accepted me for who I was, for better or for worse. In return, I shielded her as much as possible and kept other stuff from her. There were times when it was obvious I had been involved in an altercation, but she never asked questions. I am grateful for her trust and her understanding.

It would be nice to end the story here and say that I had finally learned my lesson and that I lived happily ever after. However, the sad truth is that there are so many more chapters of chaos, violence and, occasionally, some football, to come. The bottle wasn't ready to give me up just yet.

9
Pig Sick

Despite all my off-field problems, Blackpool were on a roll and only a catastrophic implosion could stop us winning promotion. We had been in the top three for most of the campaign and we had also added experience and creativity in the form of winger Andy Preece, who arrived from Crystal Palace for £225,000. I can't say I took to the lad, which is odd considering that today he's probably my best mate. I remember playing against him for Plymouth when he was at Stockport County and they had big Kevin Francis as his strike partner. Shortly after that game, I signed for Blackburn, apparently on the back of my performance against Preecey. That's something I like to remind him of from time to time.

So with things running smoothly as we entered February, we headed off for a team-bonding exercise after a game had been called off because of bad weather. Sam was a great believer in taking the lads away from time to time and we'd already been abroad for a winter break in Majorca as well as having been on a couple of outward-bound days, paint-balling and quad-bike riding around Oyston Manor. The football culture of that time meant that we'd inevitably finish off with a big drinking session, although to my relief none of them ended up with anything but a sore head and a good laugh.

Although we were second in the table, we had lost against Bournemouth the week before – our first league defeat in maybe ten games – so we were keen to have a break and get our focus back. We headed off for a few rounds of golf in the Forest of Arden, but, in truth, the golf just got in the way of the piss-up. On the first day we had eighteen holes and headed for the bar and what would be a monster session. We had a few swift ones to get the night going before heading back to our rooms to get changed. Then it was off to find the nearest pub.

There was a nightclub attached to the hotel and with it being mid-week we decided to spend the night there rather than traipsing down the darkened country lanes. It was fantastic. Just the lads having terrific banter and ripping each other to shreds, as you do when you've had a few jars. We ended by having more drinks back at the hotel bar and there were at least ten of us who stayed up into the wee small hours, all sat around a roaring fire due to the freezing temperatures outside. The fire was the size of a five-a-side goal, and, as time wore on, we started taking the piss out of Tony Ellis and Preecey because they weren't scoring as many as they should have been. We began throwing cushions into this open area near the fire to demonstrate how we thought our strikers should be attacking the ball. Micky Mellon was doing the crossing and our centre-half Dave Linighan, who was reasonably sober, could see where this was heading and got up to calm everyone down. But as soon as Linny got in front of the fire, he unwittingly became a makeshift five-a-side keeper. We bombarded him with soft furnishings but he proved equal to the task, tipping those cushions round the corner and making reflex stops. He was playing a blinder in fact, until, that is, a perfectly struck cushion appeared to be heading for the top corner of the fire. Desperate to keep a clean sheet he dived full length and pushed that cushion round the fire, smashing a table full of glasses in the process. It was one of the best saves I had ever seen. Linny's heroics were in vain because, during the course of the evening, we still managed to set the carpet on fire in two places and caused damage to the tune of £3,500.

Meanwhile, amid the mayhem, I had my eye on a wooden pig sat in the corner of the bar, thinking what a great mascot it would be for the club. I went across and put it on our table, where the general consensus was it was coming home with us. Darren Bradshaw and I smuggled it out of the pub and we took it back to Blackpool, in the expectation that the porker would be a lucky charm in our promotion bid. We stuck a tangerine scarf and a club shirt on it and placed it in the corner of every changing room we played in from then on. It worked. We went on an unbelievable run: winning eight, drawing two and pulling five points clear at the top, ahead of second-placed Swindon. With seven games to go, we were also ten points clear of Crewe in third and three wins in our last seven would have guaranteed promotion. It seemed there was no way we could fail, but we were hit by two massive blows.

The first involved a clash of personalities between me and Eric Nixon.

The other was losing the pig.

I can't tell you how much that pig meant to the lads and, as far as we were concerned, that was the reason we were doing so well. Footballers are a superstitious bunch at the best of times but three weeks into our fantastic run, Sam called me into his office to ask where our talisman had come from. I told him we had borrowed it for a while. Sam smiled and held up a piece of paper.

'I've got a letter here from the Forest of Arden threatening court action if we don't return the pig immediately,' he said.

Apparently, the pig had been there from the first day the hotel opened. It was a specially commissioned sculpture that had been shipped over from Africa.

'The pig's got to go back,' he insisted.

'It can't,' I replied. 'Let me talk to the lads and then I'll call the hotel to see if we can buy it.'

The lads were gutted when the hotel flatly refused to sell the porcine good-luck charm. The owners wanted it back immediately and threatened legal action if we didn't comply. We held on to it for another ten days but, after a final threat, it was parcelled up and sent back to the Forest of Arden. I swear there were a few tears in the lads' eyes as it left Bloomfield Road on a TNT truck. At the time nobody realised how the loss of the pig – plus what was to come between Nixon and I – would affect a season that seemed impossible to fuck up. You will have to judge for yourself who was responsible but to this day I believe that if the pig had stayed with us we would have been home and hosed.

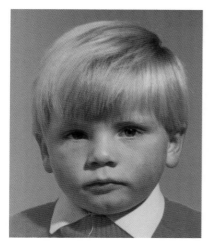

Early days. This is me aged
about five.

Kinlochbervie, where I lived until I was eight. It is the most northerly
port on the west coast of Britain and so remote that even the bank and
the cinema arrive on the back of a lorry.

Diving off the cliff at
Plymouth Hoe, aged ten.

With my three brothers. From left to right: Ian, yours truly, Cathel and Graham.

My old man at his happiest, working on the boat on Plymouth's fish quay.

Following a Royal Marines PT instructor during pre-season training. Why be second when you can be at the front?

The apprentice footballer. The very early days with Plymouth Argyle, my hometown club. (*courtesy Colorsport*)

In 1987, my debut season with the Pilgrims.

In 1992 I was young player of the year with Argyle, and also runner-up in the player-of-the-year category. Here I am at the presentation ceremony.

At Wembley for the Charity Shield against Manchester United.

Playing in the
Premiership for
Blackburn Rovers
in 1994.
(*courtesy Colorsport*)

I scored a goal against York City that might have guaranteed
Blackpool automatic promotion but because of results elsewhere we
had to settle for the playoffs.

I loved my time at the McAlpine with Huddersfield Town but it was
turbulent, both on and off the pitch.

I gave everything for the Terriers, including this header in a 1–0 win against Sheffield Wednesday.

I am pretty sure I won this tackle!

Receiving the champagne from City legend Dennis Tueart after being voted man of the match following my debut against Colchester in 1998/99.

I was so proud to play for the City fans. They were my kind of people.

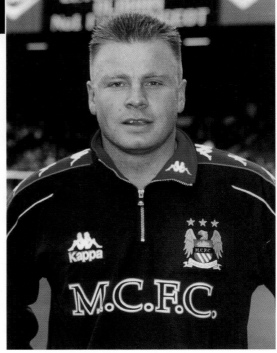

Winning the playoff final at Wembley against Gillingham in 1999.
It took City back into the second tier of English football and a step
closer to where this great club should always be.

Looking pensive. Perhaps I was worrying about one of my many injuries, or the chances of being given a new contract at Maine Road.

A great stadium, a great club and wonderful fans. My time at City has given me so many great memories.

I was plagued with injuries for most of my career, with this one coming while I was at Huddersfield Town.

My manager at City, Joe Royle, thought it would be a good idea to go out on loan to build up my fitness in the wake of yet more knee problems. Here I am playing for Crystal Palace.
(*courtesy Action Images*)

Wedding bells. With Paula on our big day.

With my son, Arron and my grand-dad, as proud a Scotsman
as you will ever meet.

With Paula and two of my children, Arron (*left*) and Brooke.

One of the world's great fighters . . . and boxing legend
Marvellous Marvin Hagler is in the photo as well!

Arron going to Wembley on the supporters bus for the playoffs. Come on City!

Paula looking amazing at our joint fortieth.

Charley starting pre-school aged four.

10

'Fucking Hell, Mozzer . . . I See You're Still at It'

We had been up with the leading pack all season and all we had to do was make sure that we didn't choke at the death. Although we were in the third tier, we were more than good enough to hold our own in what is now the Championship, if we had secured promotion. We were a good, well-organised, Sam Allardyce team with Micky Mellon scoring goals for fun and Andy Preece, Tony Ellis, Andy Barlow, Dave Linighan and James Quinn all doing the business too. But after a night on the piss, the wheels came off.

Steve Banks, our regular goalie, had made a few uncharacteristic mistakes and seemed to have lost his confidence so Sam took him out of the firing line. Eric Nixon joined us from Tranmere Rovers on loan and I can't explain exactly why but I took an instant dislike to him. He wasn't my cup of tea. In my eyes Nixon was a cocky bastard: larger than life, arrogant and full of himself. There was no bedding-in period where he got to know the lads and what made them tick. He jumped in with two feet and started taking the mick, cracking jokes and telling stories. He was far too busy for me, although having said that there was no harm to him. He was just one of those people you either liked or you didn't, with no middle ground. I wasn't comfortable in his company; perhaps I was insecure and felt threatened. I can't put my finger on it but whatever it was we were like chalk and cheese and so we gave each other a wide berth.

But I think we both knew it would have to be sorted out at some stage.

Then, an opportunity presented itself. It was a Tuesday night and despite losing 2–1 to Chesterfield at the weekend about fifteen of us decided to go on one of our infamous benders after training. In early April it wasn't that busy in Blackpool, with the day trippers thin on the ground. The pubs were quiet and it was a time when an entire team could go out for a session without it being put up on YouTube or Twitter within hours. We worked our way through half-a-dozen boozers until we came to a hotel at the end of the Golden Mile that had a nightclub downstairs, fully intending to drink till we dropped. We carried on into the early hours of the morning, enjoying some great banter. By the end of the night, there were just four of us left: myself, Nixon, Micky Mellon and Dave Linighan. It must have been around 4 a.m. when, for reasons unclear to either of us to this day, Eric and I ended up in the hotel car park. I remember walking outside and looking back through the bar window to see Eric taking his watch and jacket off to follow me outside.

Surely the captain of the club, bearing in mind where we were in the table at the most crucial time of the season, would show some discretion? Surely the best course of action was to talk things through and do what was right for the club rather than behaving like a couple of schoolboys who were prepared to settle their differences in the playground? Recalling this incident, I still regret that I allowed alcohol to play such a destructive role in my life. Because I trained hard and gave 100 per cent every time I played, I didn't feel I was letting anyone down when I lost the plot but that was exactly what I was doing. Hitting self-destruct, time and again, never learning from my mistakes. I was back behind the black veil, ready to answer the demons who were demanding I settle this, and to hell with the consequences.

Eric came out of the hotel and as soon as he stepped out I head-butted him. Before he could react I followed up with five or six punches, leaving him in a right mess on the tarmac. I had taken him by surprise, but he had come out to face me and probably knew what to expect, though I doubt he envisaged not being able to get a meaningful blow in. The boot could easily have been on the other foot because I've no doubt he can handle himself, but he never got the chance. The only good thing was that the bad blood between us was gone and we could now move forward.

Someone, probably a passer-by, must have been watching our little contretemps because two police constables, one male and one female, rolled up almost immediately. My teammate had taken a right doing and looked terrible but I told the cops it was an incident caused by drink and Eric, to his eternal credit, confirmed my account. Thankfully, the officers accepted our explanation and were happy to let us go on our way. However, we weren't out of the woods yet. Because of the state we were in, the club would most likely discipline us: Eric had a busted nose, cuts and bruises and I had an egg-sized lump on my head. The other problem was keeping it out of the papers, but as the cops had decided not to take it any further that might not be an issue.

At least it wouldn't have been an issue if Micky Mellon hadn't stuck his oar in.

As Blackpool's finest were about to leave, Micky ran out and told them he would sort everything out because he was a mate of us both. Then the shit hit the fan. Big time. As Micky approached the women officer, he stumbled into her and she toppled backwards onto her big fat arse. She must have had her shoelaces tied together because what happened just hadn't seemed possible. It was hilarious – and a complete accident – but Micky ended up being arrested for assault and taken away in the police van in handcuffs. I'll never forget his little face, forlornly peering out of the back window. You couldn't have made it up.

Our plan to keep everything in-house was fucked and the next day the local paper's billboards read: 'Tangerines' star arrested after hotel brawl!' The reporter didn't have a thing on me and Eric but Micky was in the shit. The club had solid grounds to sack the lot of us if they saw fit, but, as ever, because we were an integral part of the team, there was no question of that happening. Thankfully, the police let Micky off with a warning when he'd cooled down a few hours later and we met Sam and Gill Bridge the next morning prior to training. We were told off like naughty schoolboys and reminded of our responsibilities, particularly with a game against Oxford coming up. Eric and I shook hands and in all honesty we were both embarrassed about what had happened. As is often the way we got on really well after that and we still to do to this day. The truth is, he was never the problem. It was me.

We were in the tunnel at the Manor Ground a few days later and Oxford's captain was Matt Elliott, a guy I had known for years. He had been at Torquay when I was at Plymouth. I had gone to college with him as well and I always thought he was a great lad who made a good career for himself at Leicester in later years. He took one look at me with a black eye, and then looked at a patched-up Eric, and said: 'Fucking hell Mozzer. Things don't change do they? I see you're still at it.'

The fight didn't affect our form because both Eric and I played really well and we looked to have earned a vital point until Joey Beauchamp scored a forty-yard stunner out of nothing a couple of minutes from the end, resulting in a 1–0 defeat. After that we dropped points right, left and centre. We just couldn't turn things round. We needed six points from the last seven games to guarantee promotion, but we capitulated, drawing two and losing four in the course of a horrendous run. The truth was that we simply hit a blip at the wrong time and couldn't buy a win. It got to the stage where it looked as though we might not even make the playoffs. We drew with Swindon and then lost at home to Walsall on a day when we could have gone up. Our only saving grace was that the teams around us didn't taking advantage of our plight.

We went into the last game of the season needing to beat York City, which would have given us a chance of going up automatically. We had to rely on other results going our way and, at last, we discovered how to play football again. I scored in a 2–0 win and we waited to hear how the other sides around us had gone on. Just our luck, they all won and it had been too little, too late. We missed out on automatic promotion by a whisker with Oxford and Swindon going up instead. However, there was no time to mope. We were in the playoffs and so had to regroup quickly for the two-leg semi-final against Bradford City. With that final-day win against York we felt we had turned the corner and that we were still masters of our own destiny. Three good performances and we were going up. It was as simple as that and, with the first leg away at Valley Parade, we knew that if we did the business at their place we would be in with a great chance of reaching the final.

We travelled to West Yorkshire in good spirits with a full-strength team and turned in a performance worthy of champions, beating Bradford 2–0 with goals from Mark Bonner and Tony Ellis. We returned to the dressing room and started to celebrate because in our minds we were already at Wembley. We had been terrific at home all season and nobody had turned us over on our own patch so we felt justified in feeling we had one foot in the final. The problem was that we acted like the second leg was a formality as we shouted, sang and banged on doors, fully aware that our triumphalism was clearly audible in the home dressing room next door. It was part relief, part arrogance, part naivety. Pleased with ourselves and having ripped their lads to shreds on the pitch we rubbed their noses in it, took the piss and showed them no respect whatsoever. We travelled home totally oblivious to the massive incentive we had just given their lads.

I honestly believe there was no way Bradford would have come back if we had treated the result at Valley Parade as though it was half-time. But they were up for it at Bloomfield Road, desperate to ram the singing and boasting down our throats and watch us choke on it. If that wasn't incentive enough, they opened the matchday programme before the game to find directions to Wembley and ticket information for the final! Talk about taking the piss. After that, as you can imagine, they didn't need a team talk and they came at us right from kickoff. In fact they should have been two up in the first five minutes but were denied a blatant penalty after Dave Linighan pulled one of their lads down in the box and then seconds later there was a one-on-one that Nixon did well to nullify. That should have been the wake-up call we needed, but we didn't respond at all and ended up losing 3–0.

It was a disastrous result for the club, and for Sam, and we sat in the dressing room afterwards unable to take in what had happened. It was surreal and we could hear their dressing room going bananas. They let us know in no uncertain terms what turning the tables meant to them and rightly so. They had turned their anger into a powerful thirst for vengeance. The next day we came in, collected our weight programme and training schedule for the summer and then got as far away from Bloomfield Road and Blackpool as possible. Being around the place reminded us of what an almighty fuck up we'd made and that was the last thing any of us needed.

I headed back to Plymouth with Paula and Arron to see our family and friends for a few weeks and I tried to forget Bradford and relax as best I could. It was too late for Big Sam, however. He was sacked by Owen Oyston – who by then was serving a four-year sentence in jail for rape – despite Sam being the best manager the club had had for many years. He deserved better and perhaps we, as players, could have done better by him. I certainly could have done better. As ever I put my own role in his demise under the microscope and although I had never let him down on the pitch, off it, as captain, I knew I couldn't say the same. The Nixon and Micky Mellon episodes, the High Court case and our behaviour after the win at Valley Parade all contributed to us missing out on promotion. Nobody felt more responsible than I did.

In future years, Sam would prove beyond all reasonable doubt that the Blackpool board had made a massive mistake. At the time I was gutted for him because he believed in me and helped me get my career back on track. I knew I'd have problems motivating myself to play for anyone else so when I received a call from Gill Bridge telling me Blackpool had accepted an offer from Huddersfield Town, I was interested straight away. I tried calling Sam but couldn't get hold of him so I figured his phone must have been a club mobile that he was no longer using. I was playing golf at China Fleet golf-and-country club when Gill called so I finished the round first and then called her right back. I listened to what she said – Huddersfield had bid £500,000 – and as they were in the division above Blackpool, and Sam had gone, it seemed like a good move all round.

I had a clause in my contract that stipulated I would receive 10 per cent of any profit above the £250,000 Blackpool had signed me for. It meant that I stood to make an extra £25,000 from the move but Gill said that the clause had become a problem because of the Seasiders' financial problem. She asked if I would accept 5 per cent instead. That got my back up and I flatly refused to consider her proposal. One thing I fucking hate is sales ploys and people who try and shave a bit off here and there without any real justification. Just pay me what I'm worth and what has been agreed to and get on with it. I'll go and break my leg and give you my all every Saturday so why sell me short? At the end of our conversation I said, 'No thanks. I'll stay.' I hung up and switched my phone off. I knew they were desperate to get me out and get the money in so I was in a position of strength. There were two other important factors: firstly, I was a loose cannon and, secondly, I had been Sam's player. So the chance to cash in on me was one that was too good to turn down from the club's point of view. I got home a few hours later and switched my phone back on to find about ten missed calls from Gill.

I loved the Blackpool fans and when news of the deal broke in the local paper it became evident that they thought a hell of a lot about me, too. They made their feelings clear to the club and planned protests and all kinds of demonstrations about my proposed sale. I think it was because they had bought into me as a person and the way I was. They seemed to love the fact I defended myself against three guys and put two of them in hospital. That's what fans are like and they wanted the captain of their club to be a warrior, someone you didn't mess with. I had never courted that kind of attention or tried to use it as a badge of honour. My only imperative was to be totally committed on the pitch, to lead by example and in the process fire up my teammates. I was making plenty of mistakes outside of football but none of them were intended to impress supporters. When I drank, it invariably meant there would be trouble and all the lines I wasn't meant to cross as the captain of a team were crossed without any consideration of how it might affect my career. So I was lucky because the fans loved it. I can't say I did, but I appreciated their loyalty, which meant everything to me.

Had Sam stayed, I would have, too, but now was the time for a new challenge. The truth was that once the offer came in I was always heading for the exit. Too much had happened at Blackpool. I needed to move on. It was best for all concerned and, when I figured that they had already paid me a signing-on fee and repaid my court costs – it was meant to be one or the other, not both – accepting 5 per cent still meant I was ahead on the deal. A day or so later, I reneged and told Gill I would move on after all. I packed an overnight bag and headed up the M5 to meet Brian Horton. I had every intention of returning home as a Huddersfield Town player.

Maybe the Yorkshire air would suit me.

11

Terrier by Name . . .

I liked Brian Horton from the moment I met him. He told me he'd tried to sign me a couple of times before, but, because I never had proper representation, I didn't get to hear about some of the clubs that had been interested in me until it was too late. For example, Wolves had all but agreed a deal with Plymouth, while Celtic had agreed a fee with Blackburn. Although I enjoyed negotiating my own deals, not having an agent backfired on me and, if I was starting again, I would definitely have someone in my corner.

Horton had an aura of steeliness about him and, when he talked to you, he looked you in the eye. I felt I could trust him and that was good enough for me. His offer was more than fair: a three-year deal worth £1,250 per week with a £25,000 signing on fee plus a £100 per week rise each season. I accepted it.

He also told me that Andy Payton and Marcus Stewart were joining, and that we would all be presented to the press the next day. The most important thing for me was that I wanted to play for him. He didn't have to sell Huddersfield and, after I had spoken to Brian, Big Sam called me on my way to the hotel Paula was waiting for me at.

'I see you're on your way to Huddersfield. That's a pint you owe me,' he said.

Apparently Horton had called up Sam and asked me what I was all about, on and off the pitch. Clearly, Sam had given me a good reference. It was good to hear from him again and typical of him to help someone out if he had the chance. Sam had told Brian that he would happily have paid £500,000 for me and added that if I could be kept out of the pub and got my life sorted out, they would be buying a top player and a great leader; one who could go on and play in the Premier League. Ironically, Bradford City – the catalyst for Sam's dismissal and my leaving Bloomfield Road – came in with an offer of £350,000 before I signed, but Gill Bridge didn't even bother telling me about that. Huddersfield had done their homework, didn't try to get me on the cheap and as a result had their bid accepted.

The Blackpool fans let the club know they weren't happy with my sale, swamping radio phone-ins and writing to the chief executive and chairman. I got a load of letters from fans begging me to stay, but it was clear they wanted to cash in on me: the fights, the court cases and missing out on promotion in such sickening circumstances meant that a move was best for everyone. I needed to leave all that behind and move forward, but little did I know there would be more problems lying ahead of me at the Alfred McAlpine stadium.

We moved to Worksop because it wasn't a million miles from the ground and because Darren Bradshaw, a good mate who was still at Blackpool, lived there. Paula got on well with Darren's wife and I thought it would be best if she had a friend nearby. It meant a forty-minute drive to training every day, not the end of the world, but a chore nevertheless.

Horton had asked me to take the skipper's armband and while it was an honour to be asked, it is an issue that needs to be handled sensitively. Lee Sinnott had been the captain for a few years and was a great professional and a really nice guy who was respected by the players and the fans. Brian, however, wanted to go with his own man and because he had signed me to provide leadership on the pitch, it made sense.

Marcus, Andy and I amounted to £2 million-worth of new talent, big money for a team in the second tier of English football. It represented a new era for the club, which was showing the determination and ambition needed to get into the Premier League. As we were staying at the same hotel we had dinner together, along with our wives. Andy was a quiet guy whereas Marcus was a bit of a farmer's lad from Bristol and we got along straightaway. After the meal we went our separate ways for a fortnight before we met up again for pre-season training.

It was a bit strange on my first day because I had been given the captaincy without knowing any of the lads. I felt uncomfortable because I knew how I'd feel if the same thing had happened to me – in fact it would do later in my career – but that was just the way it was and I knew the awkwardness would pass. We had a few training sessions before heading off to Ireland on a team-bonding trip and to play a few pre-season games. There was no drinking or socialising, which was fine and as it should have been. I could see that the regime at Huddersfield was going to be a lot stricter than it had been at Blackpool, but maybe I needed that.

We returned home without incident and upped our sessions with the season just days away. I made my debut against Sheffield Wednesday in the last pre-season friendly and I got off to the prefect start, sending a thumping header into the net and running off to celebrate with our fans in the corner. It turned out to be the only goal in a 1–0 win. I couldn't have asked for a better start to life with the club and, yet again, I had managed a goal in my first game for a new club. Our opening league game was against Charlton and we won again, by two goals to one. I scored the winner with a header from Rob Edwards's corner, having out-jumped Richard Rufus to plant the ball home. Once again, I ran off to celebrate with the fans and had to pinch myself because of the incredible start I had made. Another winning goal and an instant bond with the Huddersfield public. It wasn't just about me; there was a good team spirit in the squad so the early signs were promising.

Our next game was away to Barnsley, but despite going 1–0 up (from a goal I spuriously claimed, after saying I'd got a touch from a long throw) we still lost 3–1 and were brought down to earth with a bump. We then drew against Crystal Palace before I became a father for the second time with the birth of our first daughter, Brooke, who made her appearance on 6 September 1996 at Bassetlaw hospital, Worksop. It had been touch and go whether I travelled to the League Cup game against Wrexham in midweek because Paula was due at any moment, but she insisted I played. After the game I went straight to the hospital to see her and, fortunately, she hadn't gone into labour.

Then, two days later, I went to the hospital after training to be told Paula was nowhere near ready to give birth and to go home and get some rest as I had a game the following day. Paula was fine with that so I got in my car and drove home. I was no more than five minutes away from the hospital when I got a call to say I was a dad again and that Paula had had a baby girl. It was as quick as that. I was, as the football cliché has it, over the moon and now I had a little girl to dote on as well as Arron, who was by that time three and into everything. I played the next day floating on air and played my part in a great 3–1 win over Ipswich. Little did I know that I'd soon be able to help Paula out with our new arrival more than either of us had envisaged.

We had made a great start to the season and a win over our next opponents, Tranmere, would put us in the top three. But forty minutes into the game, I went up for a header and felt a sharp pain in my left knee, which stopped me from being able to jump. I carried on until half-time and told the physio this was a new pain, something I'd not had before. Whatever it was, it felt wrong. Five days later I was under the knife with my femoral conidial drilled, cartilage trimmed in my knee and a piece of floating bone taken out of my ankle.

Just like at Blackburn, I don't think the club were happy that I needed surgery so soon after signing, but nothing had been picked up by the medical and I hadn't fudged it this time. I was ruled out for seven weeks and then came back to light gym work, followed by full training again, as I slowly built up my fitness. After a couple of months out, I was nearing a return but still needed a couple of reserve games under my belt to sharpen my fitness up. We had Manchester City next and the gaffer asked how I was and whether I would be able to play. I told him I hadn't played a game since returning to training so I wasn't 100 per cent, but assured him that I would love to play if he needed me. He said he did and so I came back into the first team for the game at Maine Road. I played for about seventy-five minutes and then came off, more because of fatigue than pain, and watched from the bench as Ian Lawson missed two great chances to win the game in the last two minutes. We drew 0–0, which was a good result for us, but the following day my knee was badly swollen and after speaking with a specialist, it was decided that I should have another operation. There was loads of damage in my knee and the places that had been drilled to stimulate more growth had actually come away and there was now a hole where they had been. I was looking at the prospect of three months on the sidelines, which was a disaster for me because it meant I would have been out of the team for the best past of six months by the time I returned to full fitness. More worryingly, it was obvious that my knee was deteriorating and would only get worse in the future.

I had the operation and built up my fitness slowly but surely. In my absence, the team was blowing hot and cold and it seemed to me that the pressure was telling on the gaffer, who also had one or two personal issues to deal with away from football. It wouldn't be long before we clashed.

After we had treatment in the mornings, me and the other injured lads would wait for the rest of the squad to go out training before visiting the wash room where Jeannie – who washed and prepared the kit – would make us bacon sandwiches. On one occasion there were three of us in there, tucking into our bacon sarnies when the gaffer walked in looking for his training top. It wasn't the best scenario, especially when the rest of the lads were outside training hard in the wind and rain. Brian flipped. After uttering a couple of threats, he grabbed his top and slammed the door on his way out. Sam Collins came in a few seconds later and when the other injured lad warned him that the gaffer was on the warpath he opted not to take the bacon-and-egg sandwich he had ordered five minutes earlier. When Jeannie handed it to him he said, 'I'm not having that now. Not after that. He'll go fucking mental.'

I challenge any man worth his salt – especially a Scot or a fisherman – to turn down a bacon-and-egg sandwich. Sam had bottled it so I grabbed Jeannie's delicious concoction.

'Don't throw it away,' I told her. 'I'll have it.'

I added lashings of ketchup and as I sank my teeth into that work of art, the door flew open and there was the gaffer.

'I want all you fuckers weighed first thing tomorrow morning,' he barked, before he turned to look at me. My mouth was full, with ketchup dribbling down my chin. 'Are you taking the fucking piss out of me?' he asked.

Without thinking I replied, 'Gaffer, there's an egg in this. It's got protein and is great for bone growth.' He wasn't amused. He gave me an evil look and stormed out, slamming the door behind him yet again.

I got weighed the next day and was found to be thirteen pounds over-weight. In consequence I was put on a weekly fines programme and fined £20 per excess pound until I got down to the correct weight. I paid £260 the first week but quickly reduced the fine to £100 after los-ing eight pounds in a week. I cut down to one bacon sarnie a day (ish) and the gaffer was pleased with that, telling me that if I lost the extra five pounds in the next fortnight, I wouldn't have to pay any more in fines. But there was a sting in the tail: if I put any weight back on, he would backdate the fine. He didn't need to because I lost it all. It would have broken my heart to keep shelling out for a few excess pounds but it proves that fines can work if they are implemented in the right way.

I finished my recovery with a visit to Lilleshall, the rehabilitation centre used by the England squad for training. It was my first visit and I stayed with Sam Collins, a promising young lad from Huddersfield who was also out with a long-term injury. We stayed for two weeks in a bid to speed up recovery and were helped by the intense one-to-one treatment that is on offer there. It allowed me to focus on getting fit and the change of scenery was just what I needed. It would be the first of many visits.

As skipper, I was in rehab more often than on the training pitch and I missed a total of five months during my first full season with the club. I returned for the last five games of the campaign, but I was glad to see the back of the 1996/97 season. I put all my energy into train-ing hard through the summer so that I could race out of the blocks in pre-season and make up for lost time. Things went well and I didn't have any further trouble with my knee and, after a decent pre-season, we began the 1997/98 season away to Oxford, losing 2–0. It was a sign of things to come because we just couldn't get going and failed to win any of our first ten league games. So, by the time leaders Nottingham Forest arrived at the McAlpine, the gaffer's days were numbered. We were bottom of the table and though we gave them a good game – and Alan Brazil nominated me for man-of-the-match – we lost 2–0 and Horton was sacked the next day. Looking back, he had lost some of his intensity and I think he would be the first to admit there were things outside of football that had affected his focus. He wasn't where he wanted to be but he had taken the club as far as he could, which is just how football goes sometimes.

12

The Great Escape, Parts One and Two

The board didn't waste much time finding a new boss because not long after Horton was shown the door Peter Jackson was brought in, with Terry Yorath as his right-hand man. They arrived with the team rock bottom and apparently heading for the third tier of English football, despite having a squad that should have been challenging for the playoffs. Jacko was a Huddersfield legend and a very likeable person and was taking on his first job in management while Yorath ('Taff') was a more than capable assistant. Jacko's personality, a mixture of enthusiasm and humility, was refreshing and I instantly took to the bloke. He'd ended his playing career with Halifax to manage us so it was a big chance for him even if it was a gamble for the club. His appointment was popular with everyone connected to Huddersfield because he had made such an impression during his playing days. It gave the place a lift at a time when we really needed it. On the training pitch Yorath was the organiser and coach while Jacko was the face of the club and the self-proclaimed 'best-looking manager in football'.

Yorath beasted us in training with an old-school regime of hill running and intense stamina sessions, all designed to see how far he could push us and what we were made of. We ran up and down terraces, up hill and down dale, always to the point of exhaustion. He was pushing us to the limits. Trust me, sports science was the last thing Taff had in mind but to me his methods were spot on. Modern-day football is full of sports scientists and statistical experts, but I have yet to see an energy drink or a Prozone reading that helps you win a 50–50 challenge. Taff was spot on with his methods and I had no problem with his approach because, when the pain kicks in, you discover who has the courage and strength to kick on and who is lacking in those qualities. There is definitely a place for that kind of training and it was an intelligent way to suss out the squad in the first few weeks. One day he made us do ten hill runs and, by the ninth, we were at the point of dropping, but at least we could see an end to it. 'Right,' he said when we had completed the tenth, 'I want another three'. There were one or two who couldn't hack it while others tried manfully but were by now out on their feet. It was his way of figuring out who would be able to dig deep in the battles to come and those who would fold when the going got tough.

There was no quick fix on the pitch, however, and we went down 3–0 at home to Charlton in Jacko's first game in charge, which was followed by heavy defeats at Sunderland and Port Vale. We were yet to find the magic formula and were five points adrift of the team above us, Portsmouth, although we did at least stop the rot with a 1–1 draw against them at the McAlpine. Another 3–0 defeat followed at Middlesbrough before we finally began to turn the corner with a home game against Stoke. It was our fifteenth league game of the season and we still hadn't won, but we finally managed to get our noses in front, going 2–1 up with just a few minutes to go. Sensing our nervousness Stoke threw the kitchen sink at us in the dying seconds. Their keeper came up for an injury-time corner and I managed to head it clear to Paul Dalton on the edge of our box. He beat two players but was too exhausted to run towards the empty Stoke net so hit the ball as hard as he could from the halfway line. It was accurate but it was agonising to watch as the ball started to slow down and the defenders began to catch up. The whole stadium held its breath as the ball trickled on, ever slower, but finally crept over the line to make it 3–1, sending our fans mad. The euphoria was incredible and there was a mass pile-on in the centre circle as we celebrated, with Jacko the last man on top. The relief was incredible and it gave us the impetus we needed to start what would become known as 'the great escape'.

In the meantime we had added three players to the squad: Wayne 'the chief' Allison for £800,000 as well as Barry Horne and Dave

Phillips, a player I used to bunk off school to watch train when he was at Plymouth. The new boys gave the team a more solid look. We lost at Tranmere in our next match before heading off to one of the biggest games of the season against Manchester City at Maine Road. City had been expected to go straight back to the Premier League the season before but had floundered and were now, like us, close to the bottom of the table, which was incredible to see for a club of their size, though obviously our only intention was to go there and make their situation worse. Rob Edwards was a boyhood City fan and all he could talk about all week in training was finally having the chance to play at Maine Road; he was like an excited school kid. We had done our homework and we knew that if we stopped Georgi Kinkladze playing we had a good chance of beating them, so Jon Dyson was given the job of man-marking him. He did a terrific job and never gave Kinkladze an inch of space and as a result we looked good for at least a point.

But it got even better than that.

Following a fantastic, eighteen-pass move – in the course of which City didn't touch the ball – Dave Phillips crossed for Rob Edwards to volley past Martyn Margetson for what proved to be the winner. It was a goal Spain or Brazil would have been proud of and it turned out to be the turning point in our season. If we could beat Man City away and play like that, we could do anything. There were almost twenty-five thousand watching that game and the City fans had reached the end of their tether; losing to the bottom club had been the final straw. They relied on Kinkladze to the exclusion of everyone else, simply because the players around him weren't up to the task. The tension inside the ground had been tangible and I'd been up against a lad called Barry Conlon, whom I'd totally dominated. To me Conlon was never a City player, although did go on to enjoy a long career . . . with the likes of Darlington.

We were still celebrating in the dressing room when a steward came in and told us it could be a while before we would be able to leave because of a mass protest outside the main entrance. A mob of three thousand were trying to break down doors to get at chairman Francis Lee or manager Frank Clark – I'm not sure which – and it was the first time I had come across the City fans and witnessed their passion and frustration up close and personal. The police eventually calmed things down, dispersed the crowd and we went on our way, but the events of that day left an impression on me. It was something I would never forget.

We beat Reading at home in our next game as we gradually began to edge towards the teams above us and then went on a bit of a run, losing just two of our next nine games. The Chief chipped in with a few goals and Phillips was a classy midfielder who made the team tick, but, while Barry Horne was a decent addition, I had an issue with him because he'd broken Leigh Cooper's leg about fifteen years before while he was playing against Plymouth. Leigh had been one of my favourite players, clocking up close to four hundred appearances over a ten-year period, and, at the time, I was gutted for him. It had been a hard, full-blooded challenge but it pretty much was the end of the road for Leigh. During a drink with Barry I mentioned that he had all but ended the career of one of my heroes. He recalled the incident straightaway.

'Bloody hell, you don't forget much, do you?' he said, taken aback. 'Christ yeah, I remember that. It was a horrific tackle. I completely mistimed it.'

That was what I wanted to hear and I got along well with Barry after that.

Meanwhile, Jacko had changed our system from 4-4-2 to 5-3-2 and I was enjoying being part of a three-strong central defence, with Kevin Gray and Jon Dyson playing slightly in front of me. My knees were still sore and I certainly wasn't 100 per cent fit. It meant that I had carefully to organise those around me and head the ball clear when required. That was the stuff I did best.

The team now had a balanced look about it and in Marcus Stewart we had one of the best players I had ever played with. His movement, touch and awareness were as good as anything I had come across and if there had been a turn of pace to go along with those attributes, there were no heights he couldn't have scaled.

So with things going smoothly at Huddersfield, maybe I shouldn't have been too surprised when my knee went again in January 1997. The piece of bone that had been repaired had come away on the medial side and that pretty much finished my season and set off a chain of events I was lucky to survive. After another operation and a few weeks' rest, I needed to go back to Lilleshall for more intensive remedial work. After about ten days of hard slog, I decided to go back to Plymouth for a long weekend to catch up with family and friends.

I had no idea I was heading for the worst beating of my life. I still can't fathom how I came out of it alive.

I drove back to Devon on the Friday afternoon, where I had arranged to meet my brother Ian and a few friends on the fish quay. As was the custom, whenever we were in for a long session, we would start off by necking pints of scrumpy in the Dolphin. It was 9 per cent volume and had bits of wood in the bottom that you had to sup. We knew where it was going to take us but I still downed three pints before we moved on. Next on our itinerary was a pub crawl around the Barbican, before we ended up, as planned, at the Sea Angling Club, where most of the fishermen finished their nights out. It was members only, but Ian worked a number of doors in the city and promised he would get us in. None of us fancied going down to Union Street so it seemed the obvious choice.

I hadn't been in any Plymouth clubs for a year and there was a new security firm working there, so the usual skip past the queue, handshake with the bouncers and walk straight in was met instead with an arm across Ian's chest.

'It's okay, I know Ivor,' Ian said, referring to the guy who ran the place.

'Yeah?' replied the bouncer. 'Well I don't know who you are, mate.'

Ian's face was a mixture of embarrassment and anger. He asked if he could see Ivor, and eventually he came out and told the doormen, 'Yeah, they're okay, let them in.' As we went in, Ivor added, 'A quiet night, eh lads? No hassle.'

Ivor knew only too well that we'd had a skinful. He also knew the possible consequences of letting us loose inside his place, but he was probably more concerned about how we would have reacted had entry been refused. He stuck around for a few minutes, asking how things were at Huddersfield and how I was fitness wise, but I could sense that Ian was on one. He had been shown up outside and was not going to let a snub like that pass off without retribution. Those words – 'I don't know who you are' – would be eating away at him and the lack of respect the bouncers had shown him meant he had taken it personally. He had been bouncing in Plymouth for a good few years and there was an unwritten rule that guys in that line of work looked after each other. As far as my brother was concerned, the Sea Angling Club bouncers had crossed the line. He had been told to wait, in front of me and a couple of mates. It was eating him up and my instinct was to go home because I could see what was coming. The lads who were with us, Jacko and Darren Tallon, didn't stick around too long as they had drunk their fill. An hour or so passed and I was next to Ian at the bar when he said, 'You know it's going to go off, don't you?'

'Yup,' I said. 'When?'

He looked over to the exit. 'On our way out.'

There was no point trying to talk him out of it because it would have been a waste of time. I knew what he was like better than anyone and I couldn't leave him there on his own, so I prepared myself for the brutal confrontation to come. There were three bouncers near the door and when Ian finished his drink he said, 'Right. I'm gonna do the fat cunt first and then we'll do the other two.'

It was now after two o'clock, and there were only eight people left in the bar.

'Ready?' he asked me.

'Yeah, let's do it.'

He walked slowly but deliberately towards the exit and then broke into a trot before running full steam with his head down until he smashed his forehead into the guy's temple, smashing his cheekbone in the process and knocking him out cold. That fat cunt went down, convulsing, with blood pouring from his mouth. His two mates put up limited resistance and were given a good hiding. I probably overstepped the mark, hitting one of them more than was strictly necessary. The doorman who had put his arm across Ian's chest was now on the ground with Ian smashing his head onto the floor. It was brutal and frenzied. As he repeatedly banged his head, Ian demanded, 'What's my fucking name? Say my name. Say it. You fucking know who I am now, don't you, you fucking cunt?'

Ian had lost it and I dragged him off because I wasn't at all sure that he was going to stop. I told him it was time to go. They'd had enough. As we left the police came on the scene, followed by an ambulance, and we watched furtively from a side street. Thankfully, the ambulance left without any patients and it appeared the police weren't pushing it. I reckoned Ivor had told the crew he would have a word with me and try and get some money for his staff as compensation. If only a few quid could have sorted it.

Any progress I had made in sorting out my personal life had gone in one crazy night. I should have known it would end that way because nights like that always did. Just another day in the life of the captain of Huddersfield Town, who was recovering from a serious knee injury. It beggared belief that I had gambled with my career for the umpteenth time, but there was much worse to come. This episode was far from finished. My lifestyle was about to catch up with me big time.

Saturday was a quiet day. I went to watch Argyle at Home Park and had a quiet night in. Sunday was a different story. I had arranged to have a game of snooker with Darren Tallon and then have a couple of pints afterwards. We were enjoying the craic and decided to make a night of it and so we headed down to Union Street to a place that used to be called Diamond Lil's for a late drink. As I walked through the single door to the desk where they sold the tickets, I noticed a guy with a huge black eye, but recognised him too late. Next to him was a guy called Tony Tasker, who I'd been at school with and who was now running his own door firm. Darren was grabbed, thrown out of the club and the door was then bolted. The three guys we had beaten up on Friday were part of a sixteen-strong firm, whose night out happened to be on that Sunday in that club. Talk about walking into the lion's den. It was akin to a suicide mission, except I had no idea that I'd embarked on one. My heart was in my mouth because I knew there was a good chance that I wouldn't get out in one piece, and, even if I did, it could easily be the end of my playing career and God knows what else. Four more bouncers came over from the bar area, one of them being the brother of the lad I'd fought with at the Sea Angling Club. He took a swing at me but missed and fell over. I grabbed hold of him and turned to Tasker, who wasn't involved in the violence, and asked: 'Do I get a chance, here?' but he just turned away. They must have thought it was Christmas, me blundering in like that. Now they could take their revenge.

The rest of them came at me from behind, knocked me to the ground and started beating me with baseball bats. I was kicked, bottled on the head and slashed with a Stanley knife across the back of my hand, a cut that severed a finger tendon. My ordeal lasted what seemed like an eternity and at one point I tried to play unconscious but, as I lay there, another bottle was smashed across my forehead and then I was stabbed in the back of the head with another broken bottle. It was merciless and I was bearing the full brunt of their anger. If I had blacked out, I would have been killed because I don't think I could have taken too many more blows to the head and an undefended whack might just have finished me off. As it was, I somehow scrambled up and managed to break free and stumbled out of a side door.

I was in a bad way and tried to flag down a passing car but I must have looked a right state. I crossed the road and was aware that three of the bouncers were following me, baseball bats in hand. Hadn't I had enough? Apparently not. I staggered over to a back lane off Union Street, soaked in blood and in agonising pain. My jaw was broken, my cheekbone was fractured and I had four broken ribs and could barely breathe, yet I was running for my life. I couldn't go any further. I scrambled into an industrial bin and pulled some bin liners over me and just waited. I heard them pass once with the bats dragging on the floor, then they came past again but, thank God, they then gave up the ghost. The pain was incredible and after about three minutes I clambered out of the bin and staggered towards the streetlights. I was drifting in and out of consciousness before collapsing and blacking out completely. I woke up eighteen hours later in Derriford hospital. It turned out that a taxi had almost run me over as I lay in the road and the driver had called an ambulance. I had a brain scan at six o'clock that morning and my head, which is big anyway, was grotesquely swollen, to twice its normal size. I was stitched up and taken to theatre for micro-surgery on my hand and had a string attached to my finger while it healed. I needed seven stitches in my head and sixteen more in my hand where the tendon had been reattached.

My dad came in to see me at eleven that night and I could just about see him out of the corner of my eye, which was swollen and all-but shut. Ian came in, too, and took a photograph of me. It was horrific. I couldn't speak because my jaw had gone but I heard Dad say, 'Andrew, dear God, look at you.' He held his head in his hands and I could see that his eyes had filled up. It was only the second time in my life I'd seen him like that so I knew I must have been in a bad way. The nurse reassured him that I would be all right and that I was a tough kid. I fell asleep again and remained on morphine for the next five days until I was finally released.

The whole affair stayed out of the papers, mainly because I was out injured and the beating had taken place in Plymouth. Paula called the gaffer to tell him what had happened and I remained in Devon to convalesce at my dad's for a few weeks until I healed up enough to go back to Worksop. I recovered pretty quickly but my ribs, jaw and hand took a bit longer to heal. Then, when the swelling and bruising had gone, I started to look half human again.

The police arrived at Dad's a fortnight later to tell me they had closed-circuit-television footage of the bouncers looking for me with the baseball bats but that the footage inside the club had been wiped clean. They had names and felt there was enough evidence for a conviction. They asked me if I wanted to proceed. But I didn't. It wasn't about being heroic or a code of silence, it was just the way it was. I'd been involved in dishing out a beating and that incident hadn't gone any further so this episode was over too. I had no intention of helping the police and their threats about making me cooperate fell on deaf ears. Further down the line, four of the six lads who'd done me beat someone else to a pulp in a takeaway and were sent down for two years.

About a month later, I got a message from Tony Tasker asking me to go and meet him on Union Street, which I did. I didn't go into the club but stood at the door and asked him what he wanted. There was no way I was going in.

'Look, I just wanted to say you don't have to worry about coming into town. And your brothers don't have to worry, either. I know the police have been trying to do us and you won't press charges so it's over and they won't be having any trouble from us.'

I just wanted an end to it, but it was reassuring to know that my brothers wouldn't have any problems because they lived in the city and I didn't. I returned to Huddersfield to begin my rehabilitation and resumed my career as though nothing had happened. Another chapter in the Andy Morrison saga had been closed.

I managed to get back to full fitness and wanted to play again as soon as possible. I had played a part in our survival, even though I had been out for four months. With a couple of games to go, we were safe. From a psychological point of view, I asked Jacko if I could play in the last match of the season so I didn't have to wait until August to feel part of the team again. He thought it was daft to risk picking up an injury on the last day, but he relented and let me play against Port Vale at the McAlpine, a game we lost 4–0. I didn't appreciate that defeat meant that Manchester City's 5–2 win at Stoke counted for nothing, because Port Vale's win had sent them down. I also had no idea that I had played a hand in my own destiny.

Town ended in fifteenth place and released a DVD entitled *The Great Escape* that featured me on the cover in a helmet. It was an amazing achievement for a club that had been as good as down half-way through the season. There was also a hint of irony in the title because of course I had my own great escape in Plymouth. All in all I felt positive about what we had achieved and I couldn't wait for the new season to start. The dressing-room camaraderie was as good as anything I had ever experienced. The mix of characters was perfect and I was happy to be part of it. However, as usual my positive feelings would be of the strictly temporary variety.

13

Whacking Jacko

My relationship with Peter Jackson deteriorated over a relatively short space of time. In my eyes he changed from an amiable guy to an egotistical bighead within twelve months as the team improved and moved up the league. He just seemed to disappear up his own arse and I got the distinct impression that many others in the dressing room felt the same way.

We flew out of the blocks at the start of the 1998/99 season and were top of the table after ten games. But I was already thinking about moving on as I began to feel that I was being edged out. One morning I had a trifling disagreement with Jacko during training and I then served a one-match ban for a game with Oxford United before coming back for a game with Stockport County. Barry Horne had taken over as skipper for the game I missed and we were beaten, not that it was down to Barry being skipper. I was back in the team for Stockport and as we were sitting in the dressing room about an hour before kickoff, Jacko came in with Taff. He read the team out as normal: 'number 5, Andy Morrison; number 6, Dave Phillips; number 7, Barry Horne, captain . . . '

I felt the rage building. My pride was hurt and I felt that Jacko had shafted me. He should have had the balls to tell me earlier instead of dropping a bombshell like that in front of the lads. Maybe he didn't have the balls or maybe he didn't think good manners are that important. Who knows? I'll never know and I wasn't in the mood to sit down and discuss it with him over a cup of tea. Instead I went out and gave one of the best performances of my career, simply because I was so angry. I played like a man possessed. I couldn't believe he had humiliated me in public like that. When he had been going through the side the lads looked knowingly at each other, because they knew I wouldn't take it too well.

It made me think about how Lee Sinnott must have felt when I first arrived and took the armband from him. But, while I could accept the decision, I couldn't accept the way it had happened. We drew 1–1 with Stockport and the next morning I went to see Jackson in his office to discuss the previous evening's events.

'I need a word.'

He looked up and rather smugly replied, 'I'm busy at the moment.'

'You've got ten minutes, then I'm coming back in whether you're busy or not.'

I waited, blood boiling, and then when exactly ten minutes had passed, I went back in. By now I had got wind that Manchester City had enquired about me, so I could afford to be even less tactful than usual.

'When you first came here Jacko, the lads would have walked over broken glass for you. Now they wouldn't piss on you if you were on fire, you bigheaded, arrogant cunt. I can't believe how fucking big time you've gone.'

I told him I had heard about City and he just gave me a smart-arse grin and said, 'Yeah? Well I might let you go, I might not. I'll see how I feel.'

That was the straw that broke the camel's back.

'Yeah? Well I'll show you how I feel.'

I picked up his desk and threw it and him across the room, slamming the lot into the wall. He landed on the floor with his legs stuck up in the air. It was a like a scene from Benny fucking Hill! That was the end of my time as a Huddersfield player but I felt a hell of a lot better having got it off my chest.

I marched out and went to the physio's room, where Taff asked what had gone on. I said, 'It's that cunt in there. His head's fucking gone. I'll never play for him again.' He advised me to go home and calm down, but a few hours later he called me on my mobile. He said, 'Listen, Jock. City came in for you a couple of weeks ago wanting you on loan but it wasn't right for us. In view of what's happened today with Jacko, it's probably best if you go across for a month and let things cool off.'

That suited me fine. I knew I had played my last game for Huddersfield Town. It was a shame how things had ended because I loved the fans and had been happy there. We felt we could have won promotion to the Premier League, but to me Jacko became his own worst enemy and as a result the team lost touch with the chasing pack. None of that was my immediate concern because I was now swapping a club at the top of the Championship for a mid-table League One side (it was division one and division two back then, but let's not complicate matters) which to some people would seem like a retrograde step. But this was Manchester City we were talking about, one of the biggest clubs in the country. I also remembered how the passion of their fans had seen us penned in at Maine Road the previous season. They were my kind of people.

Within the hour I was driving over the Pennines to meet Joe Royle, City's manager, at the club's Platt Lane training complex in Moss Side. Joe told me City would match my wages at Huddersfield plus add appearance money. He said that he had taken note of me several years ago when he was manager of Oldham and he seemed to know a lot about my career, right down to the amount of times I had played in midfield or at centre half and which club I had been with at the time. He had clearly done his homework and he also assured me that his kit man, Les Chapman – who had spent six months with me at Huddersfield – had vouched for me as a player and, more importantly, as a person.

Joe told me about the league City were in, what the team needed and what he was looking for from me. If I could have started playing for him then and there, I would have done. City may have been in the third tier of English football for the first time in their history, but this was a massive move for me. They were by some distance the biggest club I had ever played for. I couldn't wait to get started.

Joe explained that I'd be introduced to the press the next day, along with Michael Branch, a young striker who was coming in from Everton. A one-month loan deal was put in place and the next day I was in and out of the press conference pretty quickly. The City fans probably wondered who I was and why their team was having to take players on loan from clubs like Huddersfield Town, but that's where they were and we'd get to know each other pretty quickly. I remembered how they reacted when we beat them the previous season. I thought at the time that all they want to see is people playing for the shirt. I thought if that passion could be harnessed in a positive way there was no limit to where City could end up.

I went home after the press conference and talked to Paula about the move and she was behind me as usual. It was only a loan deal initially so there was no way we would be moving house just yet. But I had no intention of going back to Huddersfield while Jacko was there. I had burned my bridges and there was no going back. I went back to Manchester the next day to train with the City lads for the first time and was apprehensive, just like anyone would be.

The first thing that struck me about City was how quiet the dressing room was and how down everyone was. Everyone, that is, apart from Kevin Horlock who greeted me with, 'Christ, things must be desperate if we've brought you in.' He said it with a smile and the ice was broken. We would end up close mates and I appreciated somebody taking the piss as it made me feel at home. Everything had been buzzing at Huddersfield, but I could sense that the confidence had drained from these lads and that their self-belief had gone. It was too quiet and their body language didn't say confident to me. We trained as a squad of around sixteen and an even bigger squad trained with reserve-team coach Asa Hartford. The big problem Joe had was moving on the high earners – there were maybe a dozen of Asa's lot still earning silly money – but finding clubs that could afford their wages was very difficult. There were just too many bodies and I remember a quote from Joe about the size of his squad, to the effect that he kept bumping into players he had never met several months after his appointment. Within a few days I knew exactly what he meant.

Joe appeared to have faith in the younger lads. Players like Nick Fenton, Lee Crooks and Gary Mason were all getting a chance because I think he had given up on some of the more experienced pros, who should have been performing better. I joined the club when they were eleventh in the table (and remember this was the third tier of English football) and had just lost 1–0 at home to Reading. Quite incredibly for a club that had won league titles, domestic cups and a European trophy it meant there were fifty-four teams doing better than we were. That was unacceptable for everyone connected to Maine Road, particularly the City supporters. The expectancy, mixed with the negativity, made match days almost unbearable so playing the kids wasn't a bad move because fans will always cut youngsters some slack.

I spoke with Willie after the first training session and he pointed out what a great opportunity this was for me. He said if I did the business on the pitch, the fans would take me to their hearts. He added that the club could only really go one way from here and I had the chance to be part of it moving forward, maybe even the final piece in the jigsaw. Willie was a very quiet, focused and composed person, meticulous in everything he did. His training sessions reflected that: they were always oriented to the style he wanted to us to play and took account of situations that were likely to arise in the next match we played. I knew from the get-go that I was very fortunate to be given this opportunity and I wasn't about to let the chance of joining City on a permanent basis slip though my fingers.

I had a shower and went to Maine Road for lunch, which the first team did every Friday. It was chicken, beans and pasta and the lads were just as quiet when they ate as they were in the dressing room, all except for Kevin Horlock who never stopped joking and winding people up. He was a very funny lad, and popular with everyone, but this squad needed two or three more like him.

I stayed at the Copthorne hotel in Salford Quays overnight and returned to Maine Road at one the next day, ready to make my debut against Colchester United. I was nervous – more so than usual – and we piled into a bus and went to a local school to do our warm-up. This was Willie's idea and it was designed to keep the younger players away from the negative comments and pressure for as long as possible. He wanted them to enjoy walking down the tunnel and have the adrenalin pumping rather than be apprehensive at the prospect of going onto the pitch.

The fans gave me a decent reception but were probably wondering who the hell I was. In my first tackle I sent a Colchester forward into the air with a solid challenge and the whole stadium got a lift.

I had the impression it had been a while since they had seen a full-blooded tackle, but it was exactly what they wanted to see. It was music to my ears. We went 1–0 up and then, just after half-time, we won a corner on the right. I jogged into the box, wondering if I could do what I'd done at Huddersfield and Blackpool: score on my debut. The ball came in and fell perfectly for me to time my run and jump. I thumped a header past the Colchester keeper and ran off to celebrate with the City fans. Other than receiving three stitches in a shin wound, I can't recall much more but I had got what proved to be the winning goal in a 2–1 victory. What a start! I also picked up a bottle of champagne for being voted man of the match by director and former City legend Dennis Tueart. At that moment, there was a feeling inside of 'Fuck you, Jackson.' It was another example of me being at my best when I needed to prove someone wrong.

The City fans had been shouting 'Royle, Royle sign him up,' and I couldn't have wished for a more auspicious start. If I hadn't realised how big this club was beforehand, a call from my brother-in-law to tell me I would be mentioned by Mark and Lard on Radio 1 the following Monday afternoon confirmed it for me. Apparently, they said that everything was now sorted because a nightclub bouncer had been brought in and was going to save City. That made me smile. I couldn't recall anyone ever speaking about me to millions of people before and it underlined what a huge club I had joined.

I enjoyed the midweek training in the run up to Oldham Athletic away at the weekend. Again the planning was meticulous and we dealt with all the possible scenarios that might crop up at Boundary Park. Better still, everything went according to plan and we won 3–0 and I managed to score my second in two games. Only this time it was the goal of my life. The ball was lofted out of the Oldham defence and it bounced straight to me. I headed it back over one of their players to Shaun Goater, who nodded it back to me and, as it fell to my foot, I struck a twenty-five-yard volley into the top left-hand corner of the net. The whole ground erupted with what seemed like all four stands celebrating. I spoke with a steward after the game and he told me that they had been under instructions to eject any City fans from the Oldham sections if we scored. But when my shot went in the instruction came across the radio: 'Cancel! Cancel! Cancel!' as they realised there were maybe eight thousand of our fans among the crowd of sixteen thousand.

The dressing room was buzzing and I could sense the lads were looking at me and thinking that I might just be the leader on the pitch that they so desperately needed. The pressure had lifted a little but, while there was no doubt I had made an impact, they definitely needed a leader. There were other candidates: for example, Shaun Goater, but he was still trying to win over the fans; while Paul Dickov was in and out of the team. If no one else would step up to the mark I certainly would. It was a mantle I was happy to take on. Joe had been changing the team around, trying to find the right formula, so this was the first time that things had gelled. That said, it was a case of one step forward, two steps back because we then went to Wycombe in midweek and lost 1–0, undoing all the good work we had done in the previous two matches.

We then drew our next three games, mainly because we were having trouble breaking sides down. A point against City was a terrific result for the likes of Gillingham, Luton and Bristol Rovers, who would pack their defences and play out of their skins to take something from a game against one of England's traditional giants. I scored at Luton in a 1–1 draw and again the City fans were demanding that I be signed on a permanent basis. Perhaps they thought I was the answer to the scoring problem, having bagged three in my first four games! Joe said in the press that he thought I'd made myself indispensable to the team very quickly and after a training session he called me into his office. 'I've spoken to Huddersfield and we'd like to make it permanent on an eighteen-month contract,' he proposed.

I was delighted and jumped at the chance to sign. The fee was around £80,000, which suggested that Huddersfield were just glad to see the back of me. Some people might have wondered why I would swap a team going for promotion in the division above for one that was on its knees and seemingly headed nowhere. The truth was that no matter how much I had enjoyed my time in West Yorkshire moving to City an easy decision. It was onwards and upwards as far as I was concerned and I had the extra incentive of proving Peter Jackson wrong. I wanted to ram his decision to take the captaincy off me down his throat. As ever, I was at my best when I had a point to prove. Maybe that was a flaw in my personality and that desire to be the best should have been prevalent in everything I did, but give me a whiff of injustice and I was in my element and now City were benefiting.

Joe brought Gareth Taylor in at a cost of £400,000 from Sheffield United to add some height up front and we moved into December still in mid-table, but within sight of the playoffs. I was suspended for the trip to York City, who were just four points above the relegation zone and this was a game we were expected to win comfortably. But I sat in the stand as bemused as our three thousand travelling fans as we contrived to lose 2–1. That I think was the lowest ebb in the club's history because we slipped to twelfth in the table. It was time to roll our sleeves up and get our shit together. The fans had had enough and it was our job to start winning games and imposing ourselves on teams rather than let them push us around. I was injured for the next two games but we had a talk amongst ourselves about what was needed and the lads dug deep in my absence and proved they had the balls to get out of the division.

We went to Wrexham and ground out a gritty, not to say fortuitous, 1–0 win on Boxing Day. Willie called me from the team coach on the way back and said, 'Hurry up and get sorted. We need you back in the team.' Next up were third-placed Stoke at Maine Road, a match that proved to be the turning point of our season as we fought hard and finally played like a team, coming from behind to win 2–1 in front of a packed and ecstatic home crowd.

Slowly but surely team spirit was improving. Paul Dickov was one of the stronger characters in the camp, which I fully appreciated having played against him the previous season when I was at Huddersfield. Dicky was someone who annoyed the hell out of you if you were on the opposing side. He moaned all the time, was very strong for a smaller guy and never stopped working. He would nip, pull and be a little shit for the full ninety minutes, but that's what he was all about. We needed players like him if we were going to scrap our way out of the third division.

Shaun Goater was a quiet lad and something of a gentleman, but he still hadn't turned his fortunes around at City. The fans weren't sure about him and I wouldn't say he was flavour of the month in those early days. One thing was certain: he was a natural goal-scorer and he worked incredibly hard to improve his game, and for that reason he earned my respect. He always spent additional time with Willie after training, doing one-on-one sessions and discussing those areas of his game he could improve on. And boy, did he improve! Today, I look at Shaun's City career and compare it to my own and when I do I always come to the conclusion that he has the right to be called a club legend. By comparison I would fit more comfortably under the label of cult hero. I would play my part in the club's history but Shaun is ingrained in the very fabric of Manchester City FC, or at least that's the way I see it.

I was back at the beginning of the New Year and started in the FA Cup third round tie away to Wimbledon. I was up against Carl Leaburn and was having an absolutely blinding game, totally dominating him. Carl Cort then came on and I had him nailed down, too, until there was a little skirmish between us, which was no more than handbags. But for reasons known only to herself, a dippy woman assistant referee started waving her flag and Graham Poll ran over to see what the problem was. The next thing I knew he had given us both a red card. It was laughable and Joe was outraged by the decision, because it meant I was banned for three games. The upshot was that I didn't get a decent run of games under my belt until early February. I decided to utilise some of my enforced break with a short trip back to Inverness.

It was a weekend that would push me to the edge of sanity and, eventually, change my life forever.

14

Captain of City

A seed had been planted in my mind many years before about my drink problem. After I had beaten the court case while I was at Blackpool, a friend sent me a leaflet from Al Anon, which is a sister organisation of Alcoholics Anonymous. There were fifteen questions on the leaflet, which was entitled 'Could You Be an Alcoholic?'

The first question was, 'Have you ever regretted your behaviour when you've been drunk?' Tick. Then a succession of questions along the lines of: 'Have you ever done this?' 'Have you ever done that?' Tick, tick. The scoring system was designed so that, when you totted up the ticks, a score of three out of fifteen indicated you might have a drink problem. I scored twelve. A few weeks later I dug the pamphlet out again and decided I was maybe only worth five ticks, and a month after that, I looked at it again and was down to just one tick. I had convinced myself there was no problem and forgot all about it. I believe it's known as denial.

Time and again I ignored the signs. I didn't want to face up to the truth because that meant giving up the booze and I always felt I could handle it. At every club I had been at something close to catastrophic had happened, but I had sort of got away with it. What I should have realised was that each incident had been progressively worse than the one that had gone before.

While I was at Huddersfield, the club tried to help me and had gone further than anyone else by trying to find out why I did the things I did. They went out of their way to sort me out, following a rush of blood halfway through my first season. I was heading for the dentist to get some help for an abscess on my back tooth. It was half nine in the morning and I was like a bear with a sore head with my throbbing tooth. I drove down the back lanes towards the centre of town when a bus pulled out into the middle of the road, causing me to swerve and break my wing mirror. I turned around and drove at full speed after the bus. I eventually caught up and screeched to a halt in front of the bus. I ran to the driver's position and tried to pull him through the window. It was just as well he managed to cling on to his wheel because I had lost the plot.

My actions caused quite a stir, so much so that the police were called. I was arrested and charged with threatening behaviour. It was in all the papers that the captain of Huddersfield Town had been found guilty of what was technically road rage. The club weren't best pleased, but at least they dealt with it constructively and arranged for me to see an anger-management specialist in Nottingham. I couldn't blame drink this time as it had been early in the morning and I was completely sober. After several sessions, they told me that I might have a problem with alcohol and suggested a period in rehab. That was impossible because I was just returning from injury and was the captain of the team. The counsellor asked me, if I broke my leg would the club look after me? I said of course they would. His response was that what I had now would eventually kill me, so what was the difference? I didn't take any of it in but I did agree to see another anger-management counsellor, who would come to my house once a week. He discussed various aspects of my personality: what made me angry, what didn't; what my trigger points were and how I dealt with my emotions. But what he didn't address was that 95 per cent of these problems happened when I crossed the line on a drinking session. Looking back, it was all bollocks. For example, he asked me to take a notepad and jot down moments when I felt I was getting into a situation of some kind. But did he really think I was going to take out a pen and paper in a pub after five pints of Stella and write: 'That's five pints I've had now and this person is beginning to annoy me but I'm not going to do anything about it,' followed by, 'That's ten pints I've had now and I've decided to discuss the fact I don't like this twat in the car park?'

The only good thing to come out of the whole regrettable episode with the bus driver was a phone call I received from someone at Leeds City Council telling me they were doing work with kids aged between nine and eleven who had behavioural problems and would I like to come along and have a chat with them? I said I would be more than happy to help and so I went along to Chickenley primary school in Dewsbury and did a couple of sessions on how to control their emotions and remain composed. Agreed, I had hardly discovered a magic cure myself, but I did speak from a wealth of personal experience. I used situations I had come across in football as a parallel. They enjoyed it and so did I. After that, I went along a few times on my own, really got to know the kids and kept in regular touch with them. It felt good to be able to do something positive and because I moved to City during that time, there were a couple of occasions I managed to get them over to Maine Road for some lunch and to watch a game.

I took a lot of positives from that experience and I would like to say it helped solve some of my own problems, but there were plenty of issues I still needed to deal with. The main problem was that I had no control when I drank. The signs about my alcoholism had been there all along, but I chose to ignore them, so when things finally came to a head at City it was almost too little, too late. Almost.

After my red card against Wimbledon, I asked for a few days off to go back to Kinlochbervie and see my dad, but the main reason was to go on a marathon drinking session. The opening chapter of this book deals with the madness of those lost few days and how I almost finally threw my career and life down the toilet.

The fight with the bouncers in Inverness, the arrest and the night in a cell, the madness in Kinlochbervie and the thoughts of ending it all. Instead, I decided to do something I had never before considered.

I returned to Manchester and told Joe and Willie I knew what I needed to do. But I could never have imagined how finally dealing with my drink problem would change my life forever. This was something I needed to do not for a football club or for the manager, or even as captain of the team. This was for me, my wife and my kids. I had done so well at City, making the right impression and winning the respect of the players and the fans yet I had gone and done it again.

'This can't go on,' Joe said after I got back from Scotland.

'I know it can't. I know what I need to do.'

'You deserve better, Andy. Your family deserves better,' he said.

I then spoke to Willie and he made it clear that I needed to do this for myself or it wouldn't work. He said, 'People will tell you that you need to do this for this person and that person. But what about you? Don't you feel you deserve better? Don't you deserve a better quality of life?'

Nobody had ever put it like that before. The truth was that I didn't give a fuck about me. I never had and could never see a time when I would. But Willie was right. If I fucked up in the past, I always thought I had let the club down, my wife down or my dad down. Letting myself down didn't matter because I had no self-esteem.

My nerves were chronic and I was in a terrible state. I promised Willie I would do it for me, first and foremost. I had to because there was no other way. I wanted to sort my life out and to do that I had to stop drinking because while alcohol was part of my life, I was always one drink away from my luck running out. My wife had a good husband, my kids had a good dad, my parents had a good son and my club had a hard-working, committed player. But I could do better, much better.

The following evening, I went to my first Alcoholics Anonymous meeting in Sheffield. My recovery, at last, had begun. I looked up AA in the *Yellow Pages* and after training I went along to a beginners meeting, on my own, and was absolutely petrified. My stomach was churning and I felt terrible because I was coming off the back of a four-day bender. It helped greatly that I was met at the door by a guy called Gordon, who became my closest friend and guide in AA and, after an hour-and-a-half of that first meeting, I left, mentally and physically drained. It had been an incredible experience because I felt everything everyone had talked about during my first session had been about me. So much so, that I wondered at one point whether it had been a stitch-up.

The guy who talked about his life that night could have been me. He spoke about his drinking, the violence and the fear, and how he wore this mask of a fearless man, when in reality he was scared all the time. That was something I did every day, and, when faced with situations that scared me, I became more aggressive in order to deal with my insecurity.

I dropped Gordon off at his house and drove home feeling that a huge weight had been lifted off my shoulders. For the first time in my life I felt that my early death wasn't inevitable. I had accepted from the age of twenty-two that I would end up dead as a result of my drinking and, even if I didn't, I would probably kill someone else, end up in jail and lose everything. Imagine accepting that and then just waiting for it to happen? I kept blagging my way through, hoping that maybe one day, something might change. That moment had arrived. I had a chance, that was all, but more importantly, I had hope. I didn't have to destroy everything.

The following day Joe had organised a closed-doors friendly against Bolton. It was put on for me to clear my head and get back on track. I was up against Eidur Gudjohnsen, who was returning from injury, and he was a real handful with his incredible touch and awareness. I played well and, by the weekend, Joe told me I'd be on the bench for the game with Millwall.

'I want to get you back involved as quickly as possible,' he said, and, after ten minutes, Tony Vaughan picked up a knock and I was back out there, playing for City.

The charges against me were dropped by the nightclub owner in Inverness and the doorman followed suit, so I ended up with a breach of the peace and a conditional discharge. It seemed like the moment I decided to stop drinking, things started going my way. The police let me off with a caution for breach of the peace and the matter was closed. After that I followed the advice I had been given of going to ninety AA meetings in the first ninety days. It was intense therapy but totally necessary and it meant that pretty much every waking hour was taken up with either playing football or sharing my stories and mistakes at meetings around the country. On Sundays I would go to two meetings in the same day, because the idea was continually to drill the message into your psyche and keep the demons quiet.

We were 1–0 up against Millwall when I came on and we ended up winning 3–0 to complete my incredible week. I had touched rock bottom but managed to come out the other side intact. I was fit and lean and feeling at the top of my game. I was finally getting my life together off the park too.

With things going well and Joe looking for a big push to take us into the top six, he approached me to take over the captaincy. I was happy to take on the responsibility. Having been through the same thing at Huddersfield and knowing how much it had hurt my pride, it had to be done in the right way. Jamie Pollock was the skipper and while I sort of knew it was coming, there was no way I was going to take the armband without first making sure that things were as they should be. Jamie had been in and out of the team and I asked Joe whether he was he taking the armband off him or if he was giving it up. However, because Jamie wasn't playing regularly, it was never really cleared up and I got the impression that Joe just wanted a new captain to lead the team out of the division.

It had been mooted in the press prior to a home game against Northampton Town that I was going to be named captain and I arrived at the ground and parked my car around the back of the Kippax in a side street. As I got out, five burly blokes the same size as me and a bit older too were passing. I was apprehensive until I saw two of them had City scarves on, but I still wondered what was going to happen next. One of them approached me as I locked my door.

'Andy Morrison is it?' he asked.

'Yeah.'

'I hear you've just been made captain.'

'That's right,' I nodded.

'Well make sure you get it fucking sorted in there, then,' he said, nodding in the direction of Maine Road.

All five of them shook my hand, stern-faced, and went on their way. I could sense these were blokes who loved their club but had had enough of having their noses rubbed in it by that lot across the road. They were saying, 'enough's enough – let's get this fucking thing going again'. It brought home to me just what a responsibility the rest of the lads and I had. I had never experienced anything like that before.

One thing I did instil in the dressing room was the removal of the blame culture. I didn't want any negativity; no moaning, no com-plaining. If the lads saw me as a leader because of my size and natural aggression, then great, because it meant they would listen to what I had to say. While I never bullied them, I was forceful and, I like to think, effective. There was no backstabbing allowed – I made that clear very early on – and I think people respected that way of doing things. If we had a running session, fine, that was the end of it. We got on with it and nobody whinged. That's the way it had to be if we were to move forward. I was lucky in some ways because, by the time I arrived at City, Joe had identified the lads who were having a negative effect on the team and weeded them out. The result was that I inherited a group of lads who wanted to progress and improve. When we went for a run, I made sure I was at the front. Although I might have been thicker set than most of the squad, it proved that if I could be up there, anyone could. It was all a question of attitude and leading from the front. Injuries and lifestyle had stopped me being the athlete I could and should have been, but I was still supremely fit when I wasn't carrying an injury.

I was so proud to lead the team out at Maine Road and hear thirty-odd thousand people singing my name, but I never tried to be anything other than myself. I tackled hard, shouted and encouraged and gave every drop of sweat for the shirt. I never tried to be something I wasn't and to be appreciated for being me was a great feeling and the fillip I needed for my recovery. I had to compete, I had to win and I had to give everything every time I played. I couldn't just turn up and go through the motions because it wasn't in my DNA. It was exhausting to have that kind of mentality but I couldn't give any less than 100 per cent. I was aware that there had been twenty or thirty players before me at City over the past two years who had been given the chance to play for this fantastic club in front of these amazing fans but hadn't taken it. That wasn't going to happen to me because I wouldn't allow it to happen. When I got the chance, I took it. I think they saw me as one piece of the jigsaw that actually fitted. Their view was: 'right, at least we've got a fucking captain sorted'.

After that watershed at York before Christmas, we lost just two of our next twenty-four league games as we steamed up the table. In patches we played some great football but were still dropping too many points by drawing with the likes of Chesterfield and Northampton. We went to Burnley and beat them 6–0 on their own ground, but then lost 2–1 at home to Oldham after totally dominating for ninety minutes. I remember picking up a bench as we walked down the tunnel at the end of that game and smashing it into the wall out of sheer frustration.

Our momentum picked up after that and we won seven out of the next eight games. Although we were heading in the right direction, we had lost too much ground to go up automatically but with six games or so left, we were pretty much guaranteed a playoff spot. Michael Brown and Jeff Whitley had sorted their heads out and were playing really well, giving our midfield real bite in the process. Willie told me we had some talented lads coming through but that they needed to live their lives better. Joe was quite clear in the way he operated and if you weren't doing it, you'd train with Asa in the reserve squad, but if you knuckled down and showed a desire to improve and worked your socks off, there was always a pathway back to the first team.

I was in my element at City. I loved the responsibility and after every tackle or header I won, the fans chanted my name. I was in a good place, but it wasn't until years later that I was told what I was like at that time by someone who saw me before one particular game. Alan Grafton, a guy who has been heavily involved in the City supporters' club for many years, happened to be in the tunnel as we lined up before a home game. He told me I looked like a man possessed and that I appeared to be twice the size of the other players. He said that I was intimidating the opposition because my body language was saying: 'Look at this fucking lot, they're fucking shitting themselves. There's not a man among them and we're gonna fucking batter them.' He added that none of the team we were playing took me on or looked me in the eye. At the same time our younger players grew a few inches taller and stuck their chests out because they had me leading them out. They had no fear because they knew I would sort out any problems. If that was true so much the better, because it could only benefit us as a team.

Fulham had run away with the league and our only hope was to catch second-place Walsall, but they kept on winning and we never made up much ground on them. We eventually finished fourth behind Preston North End with Gillingham and Wigan making the playoffs, too. We would have to see off Wigan to get to Wembley, where we would meet the winners of the other game. We had recently beaten Gillingham 2–0 on their own ground and I recalled a few of their lads saying that they didn't want to meet us in the playoffs, but the fact was Preston were probably the best footballing team out of the four.

I picked up a knock in the 4–0 win over York at Maine Road and my knee ballooned, ruling me out of both semi-finals against Wigan so I had to watch from the sidelines as we drew 1–1 at Springfield Park and then beat them 1–0 at Maine Road to go through to the final, where we would play Gillingham. The place went crazy after the final whistle and for me the race was on to be fit for the final in eleven days' time. I'd been to Wembley once before – with Blackburn in the Charity Shield against Manchester United – but I never got off the bench. It was still the place players of my generation dreamt of playing at and had been since I was a kid. FA Cup-final day used to be me and my mates meeting up with crisps, sweets and half-a-dozen bottles of Coke to sit round a television and watch the whole day on *Grandstand* from nine o'clock through to full time.

The city was buzzing but Joe and Willie kept things really calm before the final and, while they were upbeat, they warned us of the perils of getting beaten by Gillingham. Another season in such a lowly league would have been disastrous, not only in financial terms for the club but also for our careers as players. Training was the same as it always was and we knew the way Gillingham operated and where their main threat came from in the shape of Carl Asaba and 'Fat' Bob Taylor. Tony Pulis's teams were invariably big, strong and well-organised – think Stoke today but two tiers lower – so we knew they would give us a hell of a game.

I needed an arthroscopy sooner rather than later as my knee wasn't right but there was no way I was going to miss the final by undergoing keyhole surgery. We would have forty thousand fans or more at Wembley and I was going to lead the team out, no matter how bad the pain was. I had fluid drained off my knee on the day of the game and was given a pain killer to alleviate the aching and continual throbbing.

I wasn't overly worried about Gillingham because I knew I'd be able to compete and hold my own against two big strikers. The first half was a bit of a letdown as a spectacle, with neither side willing to commit too much too soon. At half-time I had another pain-killing injection in the side of my knee to ease the discomfort and ran out ready for the second half. It was still goalless with an hour gone and anyone's game. I felt okay, but Joe must have seen something in my movement that looked a bit laboured because, in the sixty-first minute, he took me off and brought on Tony Vaughan. Joe gave me a pat on the back and said 'well done'. I sat down and just kept my fingers crossed that the lads could finish the job off, but when Asaba scored on eighty-one minutes and Taylor scored a second in the eighty-sixth minute, we had just four minutes to turn things round. Game over, I believe.

I was gutted because both goals came down the middle of our defence and I like to think that I would have prevented them, but there was nothing I or anyone else could do. We were 2–0 down and just about at full time. Half the stadium was like a graveyard and the other looked as though it had won the lottery and as time ticked towards whatever referee Mark Halsey wanted to add on, only Willie Donachie was still on the touchline, shouting instructions, believing it was still possible to come back. He was telling the guys to move the ball around and to keep playing our game and, as we ticked on to ninety minutes, Goat had a shot blocked and Kevin Horlock drilled a low shot from the edge of the box past Vince Bartram to make it 2–1. Pulis and the Gillingham bench had been screaming at the ref to blow when the score was 2–0 so you can imagine what they were like when Kev scored for us.

Then the board goes up for five minutes of added time. You could hear the collective gasp from our fans and the intake of breath from the Gillingham end as the impossible suddenly became possible. As their bench screamed, and pleaded for the final whistle, ours kept urging our lads forward, hoping for one last chance. In their minds, they had been on the beach with their win bonuses safely deposited in their bank accounts. It was human nature to assume that the contest was over and to begin partying. I looked over to Kenny Brown, who I had played with at Plymouth. He was sitting opposite me on their bench and I made a gesture with my fingers to suggest their ass was going. Then, from nowhere, there was pandemonium.

They had taken off Asaba at 2–0 to shut up shop and brought on a big, ugly, left-footed centre half called Darren Carr in his place. In our last throw of the dice, the ball was lofted forward and flicked on by Gareth Taylor. It fell to Goat, whose shot was blocked, but only into Dicky's path. Carr lunged at Dicky's shot and the deflection took it over Bartram to make it 2–2 in the ninety-fifth and final minute.

Everyone knows where they were when they heard Elvis had died and every City fan knows where they were when Dicky equalised.

We all went mad and I looked over for Kenny, who had his head in his hands, as did their entire bench. I knew that now there was only going to be one winner. With Ian Bishop pulling the strings in midfield, I expected us to win the game in extra time, but it went to penalties, though once again I never doubted we would come out on top.

The five lads who volunteered to take a penalty had my total admiration because I wouldn't have offered if I'd still been on. I would have taken one if I'd been asked, but there were others better qualified than me so I wouldn't have been in the first five, that's for sure. Kev Horlock went up for the first one and he later told me that he couldn't feel his legs because he was emotionally and physically spent. In fact, he said as he walked up to take it, he couldn't even see, apart from the goal in front of him. So the fact that he scored proved what it meant to him and how much he cared.

Dicky, the hero, missed his penalty, and had to watch as it hit one post, rolled along the line and then hit the other before rolling back out; Richard Edghill scored and then Terry Cooke made it 3–1. With two spot-kicks left for Gillingham, the best they could do was draw level at 3–3, but the pressure was too much. Butterworth stepped up next for them and hit it straight down the middle, where Nicky Weaver managed to save it with his feet. That was it; forty thousand fans went wild and we were promoted.

Weaves set off on a mad run and he was so euphoric that he kept on running and running. I made a beeline for him to calm him down. There were ten of the lads chasing him and then he came towards me, so I grabbed his shirt and threw him to the turf, landing on top of him. He was exhausted and couldn't breathe and the next thing he was under twenty bodies, gasping for air. All I can remember is

Weaves looking at me and screaming 'get off me you fat bastard'. I could see the panic in his face so I made a sort of cradle to take the weight off him so he could breathe and eventually everyone got off.

When things had settled down, I spoke to the lads and told them we had to go to every area of Wembley we had fans in and go down on our knees in appreciation of their support. We did exactly that and it was the moment in which team and fans bonded. We weren't multi-million-pound superstars who had been drafted in to save a sinking ship. We were just ordinary lads, many of whom, like me, were on £1,200 per week. But we got promotion thanks to an incredible team spirit and a never-say-die attitude.

We returned to the changing rooms and I celebrated in a different way from the rest of the lads, who were downing champagne and beer. I felt an inner calm that I had never before experienced. In four months I had gone from the pits of drunken despair to the best day of my professional career. It was a massive release and a reward for not allowing the drink to take over my life and ruin it. I finally felt I had repaid the club and its fans for giving me my life back and showing me so much faith and love. This was for them. My eyes welled up and I sat there with my head in my hands trying to take it in. Chappy the kit man left before me and I took one last look around before heading for the coach. Job done.

We left Wembley with such a good feeling that I had no doubt we were in with a real chance of back-to-back promotions. After coming back from the dead like that nothing was beyond us. There was no big party because United had just won the treble and all we had done was get a division closer to them. We didn't need that lot patronising our fans so we kept everything low key and went off and had a fantastic summer.

I had my knee cleaned out and then went away with the wife and the kids and had some real quality time with them. It was the best holiday I ever had. I wasn't drinking so was thinking clearly and not getting into trouble. Life couldn't have been better. All I wanted to do now was lead City into the Premier League.

15
Licker Licence

One thing that had been on my mind during the summer was the new deal I would be given if we won promotion. Throughout my career, various managers had made me promises that hadn't been kept. I had been let down too often, particularly at Plymouth where I had been told I was the lifeblood of the team but was never properly rewarded. Joe had promised to renegotiate my contract and he was as good as his word. When I returned for pre-season training, I was as fit as I'd ever been. I was slim, my face was drawn and my physique was one that any professional athlete would have been proud of. It was how it should have been all along.

Dennis Tueart and Joe sat down with me and we agreed a new three-year deal worth £3,000 per week plus £1,500 appearance money and a £30,000 signing-on fee, which was perfect. It was fantastic money and I signed on the dotted line without a moment's hesitation. They arrived with a figure in mind that was round about what I had been hoping for so there was no need to try and squeeze a few more quid out of the club. I felt everything had been done in the correct manner. We started pre-season by training on some university pitches by the M60 and I was flying, as were the rest of the lads. Having been off the drink for six months – and with no desire to go back to my old ways – I was looking forward to the new season.

When it came to the transfer market the club had very little money but what funds were available were spent wisely on bringing Mark Kennedy in from Wimbledon, for £900,000. He seemed like a nice, easy-going lad and he quickly slotted into the dressing room. We kicked off with a home game against Wolves at Maine Road but lost 1–0 to a Robbie Keane goal, which was disappointing, but we still gave a good account of ourselves. We then beat Burnley 5–0 in the League Cup and then it was off to Fulham.

Little did I realise that the game at Craven Cottage would put me in the headlines for all the wrong reasons.

Stan Collymore had joined Fulham and there was a lot of press coverage about his personal problems leading up to the game. He had been suffering from depression and was having a tough time of it whereas I was more than six months into sobriety and had a different outlook on life. Because of what I had been through there was no way I was going to wind him up. But things didn't quite work out the way I had planned. Right from kickoff I could sense an air of arrogance about Collymore that I didn't like. It was, 'don't come near me, don't touch me' or at least that's how it seemed to me. The game progressed and, after about fifteen minutes, he had managed to get right up my nose to the point where I decided, 'Right, you're gonna fucking get some.' I thought he was obnoxious because every time we went up for a header, it seemed to me that he was sneering, as if to say, 'I'm Stan Collymore. Who the fuck are you?'

I picked up a booking for a nothing foul on Geoff Horsfield early in the first half but was totally dominating Collymore, who wasn't getting a sniff. For someone who had played for Liverpool and should have had fifty caps for his country considering his attributes, he was completely ineffectual. Then, on sixty-eight minutes, as I was shepherding the ball out for a goal kick, Collymore challenged me. We fell to the ground together as the ball rolled out of play.

He said something derogatory, I pushed him away and the ref ran over to have a word. Collymore was barking, 'Who are you? Who are you?' in my face.

'I've got you fucking licked, mate,' I told him.

'What?'

'I said I've got you fucking licked.'

I stuck my tongue out to illustrate the point and licked his cheek. I haven't a fucking clue why I did it, but the ref came across and showed us both a yellow card. Then as he wrote my name down he realised that he had already booked me and now had to send me off. He looked embarrassed about it but there was nothing he could do and I left the pitch for an early bath.

I got changed, had a bath and watched the last few minutes from the tunnel. The Goat almost won it for us late on, which would have been nice considering we were down to ten men.

As for my dismissal, Joe said it must have been the first time some-one had been sent off for sticking a tongue down someone's throat! It wasn't quite as bad as that, but it was a shame I had spoiled things. At least we took our first point of the season, which was something. In later years, Collymore would write in his autobiography about that incident and he describes me along the lines of a journeyman centre half who liked to kick people. He must have been short on material if he needed to fill some of his life story talking about me. I didn't think Stan would need to do that in order to sell a few books, but maybe I overestimated him.

We won our first game of the season in our next game, battering Sheffield United 6–0 at Maine Road, and we then embarked on a fantastic run, winning our next five league games to go top of the table. Life couldn't have been going any better.

During the summer I had moved to Northwich with Paula and the kids and although it was a bit of a drive from Manchester, we got the kind of house we could never have afforded in Wilmslow or Didsbury. Just as importantly, we got Arron into a nice school and although Brooke was only three she too would be able to get a good education when the time came. Tony Vaughan and Gareth Taylor lived in the area, too, and we often shared a car into training, so all in all it was a good move and we settled quickly.

Because I wasn't drinking, the one thing missing was the six-to-eight week carnage, the violent release that had blighted my life for the past ten years. That had been part of the history of my life because, every two or three months, things got so bad inside me that I needed a blowout to get rid of the tension and confusion inside. So that had stopped and Paula could see I was calmer and more focused, although the old saying that if you take a drunken horse thief and sober him up, you're still left with a horse thief could have been writ-ten with me in mind. I had moved away from the violence, but there needed to be a period of healing and discovering why I had been that way took a lot longer. I didn't have to lie to the manager about black eyes and bruising and there was no need to cover my tracks because there weren't any. So many times I recall going to training, wearing my hood tied up tight because I had a black eye or a cut head, but no longer. I was just an average Joe, going to work and coming home like a normal guy for the first time in my life. It was a level of normality I had never previously experienced.

I counted my blessings. Top of the league with City; a happy home life with a wonderful wife and two gorgeous kids; top-of-the-range M3 cabriolet in the garage; material things in abundance; playing the best football of my career. Yet there was no spark to my existence outside of football and the strange thing was I was as flat as a pancake. The family routine of dad working in the day, mum looking after the house, mowing the lawn on my day off, taking the kids swimming, parents' evenings and bedtime stories; for whatever reason, it wasn't enough. My life had never been normal and I had always lived in the fast lane with massive highs and devastating lows. I began looking for a new fix to change my mood and get in touch with myself.

From the age of sixteen there had been charges hanging over me and court cases pending. I had been charged with a Section 18, wounding with intent, GBH (twice), affray, actual bodily harm, threatening behaviour and countless public-order offences. I had moved from Plymouth to Blackburn, Blackburn to Blackpool, Blackpool to Huddersfield and Huddersfield to City. I had never done 'normal' life because I was always preoccupied dealing with the shit I had caused. I was an addict and always needed the next fix, but that had ended now. There was a massive void in my life that alcohol had filled and I never actually had time to stand still and look at the man in the mirror. If I felt under pressure, anxious, fearful or had any kind of emotional pain, I never dared look into the black hole and face why I felt that way. I ran off and got drunk and dealt with it through the bottom of a glass. Some people self-harm when in emotional pain but my self-harm was picking fights. It was always a win-win situation. If I came out on top, great, if I got a beating, even better. I got off on the violence and perversely enjoyed the pain of a bust face or a good kicking. So many times I'd gone into Sheffield or Blackpool on my own, just looking for something to fix the pain I was feeling inside. I felt an air of calm after a ruck, even if I came off worst. I too was inflicting self-harm to take the torment away, even if it was only for a little while.

It usually ended with me picking a fight with a doorman and then sitting in a taxi on the way home with the adrenalin pumping and covered in blood. I had my fix and, somehow, it quietened all the shit that was going on in my head. Years later, I would spend time working with young women offenders at Styal prison in Cheshire and they told me how they would cut themselves when things got too much. Some of their faces were covered in slashes and they spoke of the release that came with cutting their arm with a blade and feeling the blood trickle out and the inner calm that followed. That is the only way I can explain the feelings that drove me to drink and violence.

I always wanted to be a regular guy, the type of guy who would take his kids swimming at the weekend. Now I was that guy I didn't want it. Although, on another level, I did. Being inside my head was often a confusing place to be, but at least I was making some progress, even if I didn't always like what I found. I suppose I was adjusting to the new reality, to the new me. But the process of adjustment was painful. Suppressing the addict inside me was unbelievably difficult. I was nine months sober and in consequence was irritable and discontented. I felt I wasn't going anywhere. There were no challenges in my life. That's where Willie Donachie came in.

I really admired Willie because he always seemed to be in control of his emotions and very focused. He had a tough upbringing, in the Gorbals in Glasgow, and was a ferocious competitor, yet always seemed at peace with himself. I decided to ask his advice. I sat down and told him how I was feeling. Why, I asked him, was I so disillusioned when things were going so well.

Willie just smiled. 'Meet me on Deansgate on Monday night if you're not doing anything.'

Intrigued, I met him and he took me along to the School of Philosophy, where he had been going for twenty years or so. I joined the beginner's group and committed to a term of ten weeks, keeping an open mind, with Willie advising me to see how things progressed.

There were eight of us in the class and we met up every Monday night and, as we went along, it quickly became clear that my mind never shut up. It spoke to me all the time. They say a wise man watches the movements of his mind but I would have needed a car to keep up with mine. It just never shut up and the tutor described this as 'the chatterbox' – or ego as it's better known. It's either telling you how great you are, or, in my case, how fucking shite I was.

The class brought home to me that I was worrying about things I had no control over. The suggested technique to deal with this was to sit still and feel my feet on the ground, trying to be aware of my body and not be the body. That would make me understand that I wasn't simply the circling thoughts that had been going around my mind for years and years. We were given different exercises every week and it wasn't about me becoming the Dalai Lama. It was about giving you the critical tools that would help you to understand that it is human nature to worry and to think the worst possible outcome will always occur. As I began to see my negative thoughts for what they were, I was able to let them go.

With all this positivity and good in my life, it was sod's law that something had to give, but although I had struggled with injuries on and off for several years, I never saw the black storm clouds ahead.

We had found momentum with a series of wins. Promotion for the second successive year was very much on the agenda and the dressing room was full of confidence. Next up were Port Vale at Vale Park for a match we knew we could and should win. I had no idea it would be one of my last games for City.

Vale gave us a tough game and were putting us under plenty of pressure, but we were winning 2–1 and heading for another three points. I went up for a challenge and felt a twinge so I signalled to Roy Bailey that something didn't feel right and that I would have to come off. It turned out to be the recurrence of an old knee injury and at first I thought I would be out for a couple of months. But it was much more serious than that.

For our next home game, Joe Royle wrote in the match-day programme that I was having a bit of an MOT, or a 100,000-mile service as he put it, but just fourteen games into the campaign my season was over. Joe also told me that there had been a couple of Scotland scouts watching me in the last couple of games, so my form had taken me to the verge of representing my country. What a proud day that would have been. For now, however, I couldn't think any further ahead than trying to sort my knee out.

In many ways, it was typical of my luck. I was at peak fitness with a clear mind and was ready to kick on and see how far I could go. The only positive news I got after various scans and tests was that the problem was on the medial side of my knee, which is not weight-bearing and therefore not as serious as feared. I was optimistic that I would make a good recovery.

The club couldn't wait around for me to get fit and so brought in Spencer Prior from Derby for about £500,000. He did well in my absence and Richard Jobson had also come in and was playing really well alongside him as we continued to win games. Jobbo was a fantastic player and brave with it, a real warrior in his own way. He wasn't in your face like me, but nothing fazed him and, but for injuries, I think he could have been one of the best centre backs of his generation.

Mark Kennedy was proving to be a fantastic buy, Goat was scoring goals for fun and Kevin Horlock was chipping in with a few as well, so the momentum was with us and around February time, promotion looked ours to throw away. It was hard watching from the sidelines and not being involved. I needed other things to carry me through that period so I threw myself into AA. I was at meetings and self-help groups almost every day to keep myself occupied and so the option to start drinking was never there.

The ironic thing was that a drinking culture existed at the club; one that Joe was doing his best to control. There were whispers about some of the lads having heavy sessions at the Press Club and Joe was getting different bits of gossip all the time. As for me, it was zero tolerance. I had gone from the worst of the lot to the most zealous preacher against the evils of the demon drink. If I heard the lads were planning to go on a bender I would tell them, 'Look, it's not right. You can't do that.'

It is not uncommon for reformed alcoholics to take that view and in fact it's an important mindset to have in order to keep moving forward. Although I was never alienated from the lads, I did feel on

the outside and drifting away a little. I didn't stop being the captain
or being totally committed to the team but I didn't go out on the piss
with the lads, which was bound to loosen my ties with them. The
squad drinking sessions would fester in the background as the season
progressed, but because we were winning games, no one was overly
concerned. You could run down Deansgate naked with a bottle of
Jack Daniels in your hand if you were winning games. It was when
you weren't winning that people looked for an explanation.

By the last game of the 1999/00 season, we knew that a win over
Blackburn Rovers at Ewood Park would guarantee our second successive promotion and it was painful not to be leading the lads out
in front of a full house – with maybe fifteen thousand City fans –
especially at one of my old stomping grounds. I travelled with the
squad to the game and was in the changing rooms with them before
they went out, but the truth was I didn't feel part of it. Ask any
player who misses out on a big occasion and they will tell you the
same thing. I remember reading Roy Keane's comments about being
suspended for the 1999 Champions League final and not being able
to feel the euphoria of his teammates at winning that match. It can't
be replicated. You're either in or you're out, no matter how much
you love the club. I was pleased for the lads and Joe and Willie and
it was a fantastic game, which we won 4–1, despite riding our luck.
It was bedlam in the changing rooms afterwards, but yet again, I was
the outsider. We went back to the Crown Plaza for a reception before
going our separate ways for the summer.

We were now a Premier League club and I was more determined
than ever to be part of it. I had two years left on my contract and I
could have gone to see Joe to renegotiate my deal because it had been
agreed that if we won promotion again, I could open talks on new
terms. However, because I was injured, I didn't feel any justification
in asking for a pay rise. By then I had an agent of sorts in Phil Black,
who offered me advice from time to time on a fairly loose agreement, but he was a pal of Joe's and neither of us pushed it. If there
was somebody unconnected representing me, they would have been
straight in there to activate the clause. But it just wasn't at the top of
my agenda. I wanted to get fit and play for City again and little else
mattered.

16

Loan Ranger

As the summer months passed without much improvement in my knee, my depression deepened. The club strengthened the squad further with the acquisitions of Steve Howey, Alf Inge Haaland, Paulo Wanchope, George Weah and Paul Ritchie. I was twenty-eight and looking to secure a new long-term deal before long because when you get to that age, you're looking at one last big payday that will take you to your early thirties. But I wasn't in a position to press for anything until I proved my fitness.

Ritchie was signed from Rangers for £500,000 and was a defender of average ability. To my way of thinking, he got the contract I should have had and was on around £12,000 per week. It was galling. He was a reasonable athlete with a bit of pace, but no more. I didn't feel he was any better than me and I think he only made about twenty appearances before being shipped out on loan. I would be lying if I didn't say I wasn't pissed off because there were a lot of new faces on big wages and, yes, I wanted some of it. I lost the captaincy, too, in my absence when Haaland was handed the armband. I never took to the guy for some reason – but was this my own judgemental failings rearing up again? I didn't feel he was either captain material – certainly not for Manchester City – or a leader of men.

George Weah was an interesting guy but I think Joe and Willie realised that it could be dangerous bringing in such a high-profile player at the end of his career because sometimes they start taking on stuff on the training ground and, the next thing you know, they have become a coach in all but name. There was a bit of that with George. He would do things in training and occasionally on the pitch that were incredible and he was a genuinely nice guy to be around. I would spend hours with him playing two-touch and have him just take me on. Why would you waste the opportunity of improving your own game by practising with a player who had been voted the best on the planet just a few years before? His touch was fantastic – genius, in fact – and it's a period of time I look back on fondly. Not bad for a lad from a block of council flats in Stonehouse!

Ultimately, Joe wanted a striker who would lead on the pitch, be a good influence in the changing room but in addition score goals for the team. I think George was more interested in picking and choosing his games as well as having an opinion on certain things. I don't think that bothered Joe, but the fact that Joe reverted to playing Dicky and Goat up front and relegated George and Wanchope to the bench a few months after their arrival tells its own story. I don't think there was a falling out as such; I think George just asked to be released from his contract, which suited all parties. He was the former world footballer of the year so he didn't want to be warming a bench. The other factor was that he wanted to progress on the coaching side and the situation didn't suit his needs or City's, so he went on his merry way with just a dozen or so appearances under his belt. Still, it was nice to get the opportunity to have him as a teammate, even if it was only briefly.

By then, I had been training for a month or so and out of the first-team picture for ten months but I had got to a point where I needed more than gym work and training sessions. Joe called me into his office with a plan, of sorts, to help me challenge for a starting place again. It was a loan deal. I wasn't that bothered as long as it helped me get back to playing football, but the added bonus was that it was Blackpool who wanted to take me for a month.

'It's a natural progression,' Joe assured me. 'It's more competitive than reserve-team football and I think it's just what you need.'

I was never a believer in all that nonsense about 'never going back' to a former club. I had enjoyed my time on the seaside and had a fantastic rapport with the fans so I had no hesitation in agreeing to join Blackpool. Steve McMahon, who had tried to sign me a few years before when he was Swindon Town manager, told me he needed a centre half so I went across and met him at the training ground for a chat.

Nothing had changed since I left, which I sort of liked, and there was a great set of lads there so everything was spot-on so far as I was concerned. McMahon was a genuinely nice guy but he was also a winner, with that streak of steeliness I liked in managers. The training was, I felt, a little dated with lots of small-sided games and keep-ball sessions, but not much preparation in terms of the teams we were about to play. That said, Macca was an ex-Liverpool player and those were methods ingrained at Anfield over a number of years.

I made my second Blackpool debut against Scunthorpe and I got a fantastic reception from the fans, who made me feel at home straight away. We lost the game but I played really well and I remember going to see McMahon afterwards and being almost apologetic that I hadn't been able to stop the rot. I stayed for six games, scored a goal and my last match was a 4–1 win at Kidderminster. I felt I was really going places, but the overall impact I made was negligible. Sometimes these things work – like when I came from Huddersfield to City on loan – but sometimes they don't.

In my second stint with the Tangerines the luck wasn't with us. There was even one game in which our keeper threw the ball in his own net and numerous other instances where we didn't get the rub of the green. The agreement was for one month and was never going to be any more than that. I headed back to City with the intention of playing in the reserves and kicking on again.

I hadn't been back more than a few days when Joe called me at home. 'Crystal Palace have come in for you with the offer of another month on loan. You'll be playing with better players and you'll get fitter and sharper. What do you think?' he asked.

Palace were in the first division, which was two levels up from Blackpool, so it seemed perfect. It was another chance to prove my fitness so I was more than happy to accept the offer and play for a London side for the first time in my career. Jamie Pollock was at Palace so I called him to get a bit of background on the club. He said: 'It's great here and a decent set-up. The training is good but the manager is a strange character, a bit wacky, and does things differently.'

Dave Kemp was a friend of Alan Smith's and had told him I would do a good job for the club. As I drove down to London, Paula called me to say she'd received a huge bouquet of flower from an 'Alan Smith'. It was my first taste of the way Alan worked and just one reason some people considered him to be a bit different from other managers. I thought it was a nice touch.

My first training session was going well with coaches Ray Houghton and Glenn Cockerill when Alan wandered in with track-suit bottoms pulled halfway up his chest and a big pair of sunglasses on. The lads were smiling and Neil Ruddock came over and said, 'See you've met the gaffer then? He's barking mad.'

Smith was extrovert but I liked him straightaway. As is the case with most loan deals, you go somewhere when the team is looking for a jump start and Palace were no different. They were in the bottom three and struggling. One of their centre backs, Fan Zhiyi, had returned to China along with Sun Jihai, so they were desperately short at the back. I made my debut away to Birmingham City and was up against Geoff Horsfield, which suited me down to the ground. Geoff was the sort of striker who bullied defenders with a series of hard, niggly challenges and other things that could easily wind you up, but I loved that because I couldn't be intimidated. In fact, I thoroughly enjoyed it. We went 1–0 up through Clinton Morrison and we were in no danger yet somehow ended up losing 2–1. Then it was off to Craven Cottage to face Fulham and that meant it was Morrison and Ruddock versus Louis Saha and Luis Boa Morte, probably the two fastest forwards in the country. So you can imagine how deep we played that day! We lost 3–1 and it had been a terrible start to my time with Palace.

Things were about to get even worse because the following Saturday we were at home to Portsmouth. Once again things were going really well and we were 2–0 up, but still ended up losing 3–2. We had now lost all three games since I had arrived but should have won at least two them after being in strong winning positions on both occasions. I couldn't work out why things kept going pear-shaped. I wasn't enjoying it because things weren't going right on the pitch but we had a chance to put things right at home to Grimsby Town in our next game. All we had to do was to get our noses in front and shut-up shop, but although we played well and dominated them we lost 1–0. But it was what happened after the game that sticks in my memory.

It was clear to me that the problems at the club ran far deeper than things not going right on the pitch. There was interference from above and, after the Grimsby defeat, I experienced it first-hand. Alan Smith gave us a dressing down and as a squad we had a discussion about where things were going wrong and what we could do better. Then, after about twenty minutes, in walks Palace owner Simon Jordan, who had come in before after our previous home games and stood at the back with a glass of wine, listening while the manager aired his views, totally undermining him in my opinion. It is impossible for a manager to say what he really wants to while the chairman is standing behind him so that got my back up right away.

After Smithy had finished, Jordan stepped in and started laying into everyone before the gaffer came back in and said a bit more. Then Jordan started again. We had been in there for forty-five minutes and I was starting to get pissed off. I had had enough and so I lifted my left arse cheek up and let out an almighty fart. It was like a trumpet going off and it echoed around the room. Jamie Pollock started laughing and one or two of the other lads did, too. Jordan didn't find it amusing.

'Who was that? That shows a total lack of respect. That's out of order.'

I told him it was me. 'What do you expect? I've been sat here almost an hour and my stomach's rumbling because I'm starving.'

Meanwhile, Dougie Freedman started having a go at Jamie. 'What's so fucking funny?' he asked him.

'He's just farted,' Jamie said, pointing at me.

I lost my respect for Dougie at that moment because in my eyes all he wanted to do was lick the manager's ass and the chairman's ass. But here we are seven or eight years later and he's manager of Crystal Palace! There he was, I thought, defending the chairman and protecting his own interests. 'What a fucking prick,' I said to myself.

I went home on the Monday and went back to Palace on the Tuesday. When I got there Alan Smith called me into his office.

'The chairman's got a problem with you and thinks you don't have any respect for him,' he said.

'Just look at it for what it was,' I replied. 'We'd been in there forty-five minutes and I farted. I didn't hold back and just fucking let rip, but that's it. If he's offended by that, he shouldn't be in the fucking changing rooms and he certainly shouldn't be giving his opinion to the players.'

Smith all but agreed with me but it was difficult for him. He was already in a precarious position so I understood his thinking, but I wasn't about to back down. I was right in what I'd said and, to me, with a bloke like Jordan you were always going to be treading on egg shells.

I finished my month off and came back to City. Shortly after I received a letter from Alan thanking me for my time with the club and telling me I had been great and that I had done exactly what he hoped I would do during my time there. That was a nice gesture from a nice guy, but Jordan still sacked him a few months later so I was glad to have left.

I had proved my fitness again but, back at Maine Road, the team were shipping goals right, left and centre. Richard Dunne had been brought in during October from Everton for £3.5 million as the club tried to find the right combination at the back, but, after a few reserve games for City Joe decided it was time to give me another run in the team. He pulled me to one side after I had played against Aston Villa reserves and told me, 'That's the best I've seen you since you were injured. You're looking sharp and fit and your weight's good so you're back in my plans again. We need to find a way of getting you back into the team.'

He was as good as his word because a few days later I was named in the starting eleven for the League Cup tie with Ipswich Town. The original game had been abandoned due to torrential rain the week before and I remember being in the changing room before the game and Kevin Horlock saying, 'Ah, the fucking big man's back. Come on skipper, get the armband on.'

Although there were new players in the team, there was still a good sprinkling of the lads who had got the club out of the second division and it meant a hell of a lot to me that they felt like that. It was even more pleasing because the current captain, Haaland, was in there, too. I could sense the lads weren't with him because of his lack of leadership qualities. I don't like to criticise other pros but, as I said, I just couldn't take to the guy. I thought he was a coward who hid in the big games but said all the right things in the press. He wasn't my type at all and in my opinion he just wasn't a strong-enough character to lead Manchester City in the Premier League. Whether there was anyone in the squad who could have done the job, I don't know, but Haaland certainly wasn't the answer.

I had a good, solid game against Ipswich but cramped up badly towards the end. Despite that, the City fans were fantastic with me and I got a reception that I will never forget. I just kept my fingers crossed that this was the start of a second long spell in the team.

I was left out of the 1–0 defeat at Sunderland, the goalless home draw with Derby County and the 4–1 home defeat to Charlton Athletic. We had slipped to second bottom of the Premier League and one of the club presidents, Tudor Thomas, told me he saw Joe after that game and asked him where we went from there. Joe replied, 'I'm bringing the big man back in. He's coming back for the next game.'

Tudor said he thought we'd be fine and that I wouldn't let him down. Joe paid me a massive compliment by going with a back five rather than a back four for our next game on New Year's Day. I was passed fit enough to face Coventry City and took my place alongside Howey and Dunne. It was my first league game for fourteen months and we played well and deserved the 1–1 draw. Once again, my knee lasted the ninety minutes and I thought that was it. I was back in the team and hoped to stay there. I played in our next game – at home to Birmingham City in the FA Cup – and had a blinder. In fact it was one of my best for City and I even scored one of the goals in a 3–2 win. The fans were fantastic, chanting my name throughout, and on a personal level it couldn't have gone any better. Afterwards Joe claimed that if I had not been playing, we would have probably lost that game.

Now I was back, I was acutely aware that I only had eighteen months left on my contract. Compared to what some of the players who had been brought in during the time I'd been out injured were picking up, my wage was a pittance. I wanted to negotiate a better deal and Joe told me the club was willing to talk, but not until the end of the season when we knew which division we would be playing in.

I was in for the next game, too, at home to Leeds United, who were flying at the time with Rio Ferdinand, Mark Viduka and Harry Kewell in the side. With the score 0–0, we got a free kick that I tried to send over the top for Darren Huckerby to chase, but I undercooked it and four passes later, we were 1–0 down. We ended up losing 4–0.

Joe didn't seem sure what about what combination to go with and although I missed the 1–1 draw with Derby, I was back for the 1–0 FA Cup win over Coventry, which was comical because after Shaun Goater notched a last-minute winner he ran over to where our fans normally were in the north stand only to find it housing three thousand Coventry fans, who went potty, thinking he was winding them up.

I also played in the 1–1 home draw with Liverpool and was up against Emile Heskey, who caused me no problem whatsoever. So, overall, things had gone really well. Arron my little lad never stopped pestering me before that game to get Steven Gerrard's shirt so I asked him afterwards – one of the few times I've ever asked another player for something – and he was very happy to oblige. I was out for the next two games against Middlesbrough and Tottenham, before playing in the FA Cup fifth-round tie at Liverpool. Joe must have been finalising the defence he wanted to go with for the remainder of the season because it was futile to keep chopping and changing. I had no idea where I figured in his plans but the game at Anfield gave me a strong indication of where things were heading.

17

Last-Chance Saloon

Too often in the Premier League we were found out either because we didn't score goals or couldn't stop conceding them. I was having a decent game at Anfield but we were losing 3–1 when my number was held up by the fourth official. I trudged off to the chant of 'You fat bastard. You fat bastard.' from the Liverpool fans and a few of them were giving me even more stick as I neared the bench. I was handed a water bottle, which I took a drink from, and then I squeezed it over my shoulder in their direction, soaking about six of them.

Of course, they can give it, but they can't take it and I had to speak to a police officer afterwards. I told him it had been a joke but then I said, 'I should have thrown them a bar of soap, too, the dirty Scouse bastards.' He didn't smile and I realised he was a Scouser, too. Fortunately, he said they wouldn't be taking the matter any further, although at a later date I did have to answer an FA charge.

I was furious with Joe for taking me off because I felt he was taking the easy option in subbing me. I think it's been well proven that the players who moan and react badly to being taken off probably get the edge when there are fifty-fifty decisions made because it's less hassle for the manager. I just got on with it, didn't complain and was therefore easier to deal with. At least that's the way I saw it at the time and I told Joe as much. He said it was tactical but I suggested there were a couple of other ways it could have been done. It was probably the only time we didn't see eye to eye during the time we worked together.

What I didn't realise at the time was that I had just played my last game for the club, although I am sure it wasn't because Joe and I had disagreed at Anfield. He told me the direction he was going to go for the rest of the season and that I probably wouldn't be involved. Instead of being at the heart of a defence that was trying to keep City a Premier League side, I was now pretty much out in the cold.

My occasional agent Phil Black got in touch soon after and told me that Sheffield United were interested in taking me on loan for the rest of the season. He also said that Joe thought it was a good idea to continue my rehabilitation by playing competitively, but it was all wrong. To me, Phil was too close to Joe and if I'd had full representation based on a legally binding contract, I think I would have stayed at City and also had them work on sorting out a new deal. I felt that Joe was taking the view that I would be needed if we went down but perhaps didn't think I could cut it as a Premier League player. I knew how much pressure he was under and it didn't diminish my respect for him as a manager by one iota.

Neil Warnock was the gaffer at Bramall Lane and seemed to be a decent bloke. He phoned me and said, 'Come over, Andy. We're pushing for the playoffs and let's see where we get.'

A loan fee had been agreed between the clubs and they were willing to double my appearance fee to £3,000, which was decent money. So I thought, 'why not?' and dropped a division to join the Blades until the end of the season. But just like at Palace and Blackpool it was a fucking nightmare. I was due up on the Monday to start training and after a weekend in Plymouth I headed back to Yorkshire with a bit of a bad back. The four-hour drive didn't help and during the first training session the muscle in my calf tightened up and I was ruled out for two weeks.

I finally made my debut against Gillingham but it was an unmitigated disaster from start to finish and in hindsight I probably was only 70 per cent fit. I felt I had done well in my previous two loan deals, but I was fucking awful on my Sheffield debut. Up against Iffy Onuora and Marlon King, I was marking Onuora at a corner but the only thing that was 'iffy' was my marking. I lost him and he scored to put Gillingham 1–0 up. We went on to lose 4–1, which was a massive blow to our playoff hopes. I had a shocker and was miles off the pace for the entire game. We were now five points behind Preston, the sixth-placed club, having played a game more. With just four matches left, it was going to take something special in the remaining games to turn things round.

Warnock didn't say a word to me after the game or after the training session on the following Monday. Our next game was at home to Wimbledon the next day and he read the team out after the session. My name wasn't mentioned. I was on the bench, which I could fully understand after my nightmare debut. I came on with about twenty-five minutes to go and did well, but we lost 1–0, all but ending our hopes of promotion. I was back in the starting line-up for the game against Grimsby Town and I had my best game yet during a 1–0 win and got a great write-up in the papers. The general feeling was that Warnock would sign me at the end of the season and that I would help the club make a strong challenge for promotion during the 2001/02 campaign.

Talk about parallel lives. I woke up on 21 April 2001 preparing to face Burnley in the first division while City were at Old Trafford taking on United. It was hard to stomach but I needed to forget the derby and concentrate on the job in hand. I played against Burnley and was up against my old teammate, Gareth Taylor, who was on loan there. Things were going well and we were 1–0 up when I sprinted back to clear the ball and felt a sharp tug on my hamstring. That was the end of my season, with twenty-five minutes on the clock.

Later that same day, I saw the highlights of City's game against United, including the infamous tackle that Roy Keane made on Alfie Haaland. My thoughts on Haaland were well-known but what I saw that day was symptomatic of the problems Joe had at the club. The team had no heart. To my way of thinking Keane's tackle was, at best, ill-judged and, at worst, reckless. In his autobiography Keane acknowledges that he was out for revenge because he felt that Haaland had been out of order when he was badly injured against Leeds a few years earlier. Roy Keane is a warrior and I can well understand that the Leeds incident would have been eating away at him because Haaland, to me, is anything but a warrior. What galled me was the reaction of our lads after the incident – they went up to Keane and tried to reason with him. You never know what the reaction will be to something like that, but most teams would have got involved to the point of a twenty-two-man brawl on the back of that tackle. Yet all they did was talk to Keane. I never got to play in a Manchester derby – one of my career regrets – but if I could have picked one, it would have been that game. I wouldn't have let Keane get away with that and I would probably have ended up on an FA charge, because it would have gone off for definite. Nobody stood up for Haaland that day. I would have done. The outcome is anyone's guess but I would have been in Keane's face within seconds and we would have taken it from there.

With no reason to remain at Bramall Lane any longer, I returned home but was disappointed there was no phone call from Warnock in the days after, either to tell me where I stood or to see how my injury was. He seemed like a decent bloke who cared about his players but I was wrong. I hadn't enjoyed my time with Sheffield because things went badly from the word go and now I didn't have a clue where my future lay. I checked in with the physios at City, who confirmed I was at least a couple of weeks away from match fitness. Not long after that, I heard on Sky Sports that Joe had been sacked.

He had decided to try a combination that didn't include me and we had been relegated. I'm not saying I would have kept us up, but I would have put my heart and soul into the fight. I have always believed that I could make things happen because things have never drifted in my life: they've either gone wrong, often fucking horribly wrong, or they've gone right. Put me in the team and I would create a situation one way or another. I thought Joe had felt the same way by bringing me back in and even changing the way we played to accommodate me, but he clearly had second thoughts. It didn't change the way I thought about him because he had been a fantastic manager for me and I fully appreciated that he had to do what he thought was right for the team.

I had a feeling there was a move to get him out because he was sacked very quickly and the club didn't hang around making an appointment. Bristol City came in for me towards the end of May and I went down to speak with them, but it wasn't the right move and I decided to stay at City and see what happened in the summer.

I still think I could have helped save Joe's job if I had been playing, but, alas, we'll never know.

I had another clean out of my knee at the end of the 2000/01 season and then went on holiday to Ireland, still uncertain about my future. I'm not sure what would have happened if Joe had stayed at City. Maybe he would have turned to me again to win promotion again or perhaps he would have let me go. You would have to ask him that.

While I was enjoying a break from what had been a frustrating eighteen months, my mobile rang and it was Kevin Keegan, who had just been announced as City's new manager. It was nice that he had taken time out to call me and he told me that he had spoken with people at the club about what was required to get us back up. 'You're in my plans and I think you're the type of character we need to get out of the first division. I'm looking forward to working with you,' he said.

He had said all the right things and I came back for pre-season with a spring in my step. Kevin was putting a great squad together and I wanted to be part of it, so I spent a couple of weeks with the physio because my knee still wasn't right and then stepped up to full training in preparation for the 2001/02 campaign. There was a group of young players coming through our academy system as well and they had a bit of attitude about them and not that much respect for their seniors in the squad, which was fine by me. You need a bit of an edge and to be able to handle yourself. It wasn't anything I hadn't done myself at Plymouth.

Stephen Jordan, Dickson Etuhu and Shaun Wright-Phillips were the main ones and it was Shaun who caught my eye because he looked a real talent in training and definitely one for the future. He's not the tallest lad in the world but, despite that, on one occasion, he came flying at me in the gym.

It all stemmed from a training session earlier in the day, during which I caught Wrighty with a tackle that was slightly late, but completely accidental. He jumped up and glared at me.

'Sorry, Wrighty. It was an accident, mate.'

'No it wasn't,' he said. 'You tried to take me out.'

'I didn't kick you,' I replied. 'You were just too fast for me.'

This went on for a few minutes but, as far as I was concerned, that was the end of it. Then later, in the gym, he walked past me without saying anything. I was on the weights and I shouted over, 'For fuck's sake Wrighty. There's not a fucking problem here. You were just too quick for me.'

'You tried to do me,' he said, so I put my weights down to have a proper talk with him but as I lowered them he sprinted towards me with arms flailing everywhere. I grabbed hold of his collar to keep him at arm's length, but it was liked being attacked by Scrappy Doo! A few of the other lads came over and took him away to calm down and I just shook my head in disbelief. Afterwards we had a good laugh about it but nobody should ever question his courage because nothing fazed little Shaun. His heart is the size of his body.

After a fortnight of intensive stamina training, I shifted up another gear and began normal training with the rest of the lads. I was selected to play for the reserves at Hyde and was doing well. I felt good and strong, until twenty minutes into the second half when I challenged for a header and, as I landed, the left side of my knee basically collapsed. I knew it was bad, but had no idea what it would mean long term. The damage was substantial but I was in no position to just accept my fate and hang my boots up with a cheery grin. Whatever it took, I had to save my career, one way or the other.

Stuart Pearce, who had come in under Keegan and was being groomed to be his assistant, was at the game and he told me I had looked great in great nick and asked how long I thought I might be out for. I told him I didn't know. Something had gone badly wrong this time but, until I had a scan, I had no idea what.

As I went in for operation number twelve, I knew deep down that this was going to be a case of the proverbial 'unlucky for some' and was likely to be the one that would end my playing career. Sure enough the surgeon told me afterwards that I had a hole measuring a square inch on the weight-bearing side of my femoral condyle. The previous holes had all been on the opposite side and you can just about get away with those because there's no stress put on them when you stand or run. He told me it would be hard to come back from an injury like that and it would be six months at best if I did.

By that point, I had lost a lot of fight and with a new crop of players at the club and the knowledge I would be training on my own, and pretty much starting again, the drive I once had just wasn't there. I wasn't sure where my future lay. I was thirty-one and facing up to the stark reality that my high-earning potential was just about over. I had no money saved because I had never got to the level where I could stick a few quid away. I had always been on deals that were just enough to live on and injury had stopped me renegotiating when we had gone up. I had to watch as a series of average players with no fire in their bellies came in, took home fat pay packets and then drifted out of the club on the way to their next big deal. That one big contract had always eluded me and now I would never be able to command the kind of wage that would see my family enjoy the trappings of a Premier League footballer.

It was a tough time but for a while I soldiered on. By October, both Paulo Wanchope and I would be regular fixtures in the physio room and the gym and I can't say we ever got on with each other. I didn't particularly like him and I don't think he particularly liked me. Paulo didn't mix. He came over as aloof and he did his own thing. To me he was the new face of footballers in this country, a not uncommon stereotype of the moody foreign import every top club seems to have at least two or three of these days. He was an individual both on and off the pitch and in my view was never a team player, but if you could have managed to get the best out of him week in, week out, you would have had one hell of a player. He had talent in abundance but he only showed you it in glimpses.

I would always rib him about his timekeeping. He often turned up late for training or a session and then, I always thought, he didn't work hard enough when he did. I would tap my watch when he came into the changing room and I told him he was no different from anyone else. I could see he didn't like it, but he would just ignore me. One day he arrived half an hour late and I looked at the physio, who shook his head, indicating that he wasn't going to get involved. So tapping my watch, I said, 'Hey. You're thirty minutes late and we're all waiting for you so we can start our session.'

In fairness to Wanchope, I think he was in a bad place at the time. He had been out for a few months and his injury was such that it had been touch and go whether or not he played again. I think he was pretty low and missing his family and he made a dismissive remark and walked out. It was two injured players, totally frustrated and at breaking point. I don't know what he said, but I was pretty sure it wasn't very complimentary. I followed him out into the corridor and asked him what he had said, knowing where it would most probably lead. He mumbled something I didn't like so I belted him and threw him against the wall. Out of the corner of my eye I saw Steve Howey passing, but he just glanced at us and went on his way, probably thinking it was long overdue that we sorted this out.

Then Les Chapman came rushing out of the kit room, while Kevin Horlock and Laurent Charvet came around the corner and both ran over to me, pulling me back. As things were gradually calming down, Choppy, who was now on his own, just ran, leapt a good few feet in the air and whacked me on the side of the head. Now I've taken some severe beatings in my time, but this was the first time I'd ever seen stars, just like in *Tom and Jerry*! I could see all these white flashes before my eyes and heard Chappy say, 'For Christ's sake, don't let him go.' It must have taken a good minute or so before I properly came round but that was the end of the matter and Paulo and I went our separate ways after that.

The incident was reported in a number of tabloids the next day, but these things happen all the time at football clubs. Sometimes they find their way into the press, sometimes they don't, but they happen all the same. We used to call episodes like these 'straighteners' and while a scrap isn't always the best option it invariably clears the air. As a kid at Plymouth I remember a few occasions when the coach would get two lads who had continually been having digs at each other and instruct them, 'Right, that's it. There's too much bitching between you two so let's get it on and get it sorted.' We would gather around the centre circle and then they'd have the opportunity to settle their differences, but they never would. They would have a stand-off and then slowly realise that it had all been hot air and neither actually had the balls to follow up on their threats. They would move on from there without any bad feeling and that would be the end of it.

With me, of course, it happened quite a lot, but one good thing was that Paulo changed as a person. He mixed more, was never late for training and he got back not only his fitness but also his place in the team. So maybe he took something from our altercation and used it positively. We didn't suddenly become bosom buddies, but there was definitely a mutual respect from that day forward.

As for me, I had got to the stage where I felt I was in the way at City and was slowly becoming detached from the club. Nicky Weaver went to America for an operation, Alfie Haaland went to America for an operation, Andy Morrison had his knee op in Crewe! And that, unfortunately, was where I was at. I understood my place in the great scheme of things but never kicked up a fuss because I accepted that's the way things were. It was time to move on. To where, God only knew.

18
Pushed to the Brink

Charley, our third child, was born on 25 January 2002 at Leighton hospital in Crewe. As with Brooke, I missed the birth due to the speed of her arrival. I had been on the way to the hospital because a midwife had called and told me to come as soon as I could but, when I got there, Charley had already been born and was announcing as much to the world. I was more emotional than I'd been before, with tears in my eyes, the works, largely because she was my first sober baby! As for giving my ever-expanding family the security we needed, things weren't going so well.

By January, with my deal running out in the summer, Keegan told me that because of my injury situation and the likelihood that I wouldn't play again, the club were willing to pay off the remainder of my contract so I could get on with my life. I understood the reasoning and after a couple of months negotiating, I was given about £70,000 and that was that. Keegan had no obligation to me and didn't owe me a thing, but he did say he thought the fans would like the opportunity to say goodbye, which I thought was a nice touch.

It was agreed that I would come out before our home game with Crystal Palace in March 2002 and I decided to take Arron and Brooke out onto the pitch with me. The City camera team had promised to film everything so I could save it for posterity and I walked out at Maine Road to the most incredible reception from the City fans. It had the hairs on the back of my neck standing up. They were singing my name all around Maine Road and it was genuinely moving. I was just glad it was being taped so I could enjoy it again and again or at least, that's what I thought. Now, what are the chances of a simple farewell going wrong?

The brief for the production team had been to film Morrison during the farewell walk and, after the game, I was handed a DVD of the evening. I stored it safely at home and didn't watch it for a few weeks until I sat Paula and the kids down to relive that magical five minutes. The Palace players had been on the pitch warming up at the same time that I'd come out and, to my utter disbelief, when I pressed play it gradually dawned on me that the guy had focused on Clinton Morrison while I said my farewell in the middle of the pitch. It was fucking unbelievable! How could you possibly get the wrong Morrison? So Clinton, if you ever want a nice DVD of you doing keepy-uppys, I'm your man. What a shame because those are the sort of things you want to savour in later years. I was gutted.

I decided that I wasn't retiring. Somehow I was going to get back playing and it was around that time I got a call from Glenn Cockerill, who had taken the Woking job on. He asked me how I was and where I was at with my fitness so I said I wasn't sure and that I might be all right in five or six weeks. 'I won't be able to give you what you were on at City, but I'll give you £1,200 a week,' he said. That was at non-league level and I tried to get my head around the fact that even head teachers didn't earn that kind of money. Where else could I do something I loved and get so well paid for it? The earning potential for any decent player is so far detached from the average salary, it was going to be impossible for me to replace.

The money City had paid me had all gone within a few months, but it didn't matter because, in my mind, in six weeks, I would be earning again. That's how we lived and that's what I still believed, despite being told I was washed up at thirty-two. I was always chasing those six weeks, but, of course, I was just in denial and afraid to face up to the truth, but that could have applied to a number of things in my life.

While I was getting my head round my playing career being over, I received a triple whammy that, even now, I can't believe actually happened. That I was able not only to handle each catastrophe as it came, but also managed to come out the other side intact, is a minor miracle. The events from April 2002 through to August of the same year left me numb, bewildered and I'm still baffled how it didn't end with me hitting the bottle again. Maybe I was stronger than I thought.

I went back to Plymouth to see my brother Ian and the family, and, for the first time in my life, the fickle hand of fate was kind to me. Being sober saved me from the tragic events that were to follow.

I arranged a night out with Ian and a few of the lads from the Barbican. It was to be the usual pub crawl and we set off early on the Saturday evening. It was great to see the lads again and the banter was as sharp as ever, with everyone ripping the piss out of each other and me the butt of the jokes, as usual. 'Big-time Charlie', 'pampered footballer' and 'Are you sure you don't want to go to a wine bar?' and all the usual crap I get thrown at me. The only difference this time was that I was drinking orange juice instead of alcohol. I was also aware that not just booze was being consumed, with one or two of the lads nipping off to the toilet at regular intervals for a quick snort.

Inevitably, the jovial mood didn't last. Trouble will always find trouble, and, sure enough, it came in the shape of a group of lads from Stonehouse, a group that we had numerous run-ins with over the years. They walked into the Maritime on the Barbican and I knew three of them in the form of the Wroe twins and David Taylor, who had lived in the block of flats behind where Dad and I lived. It was still early and there was a stand-off, nothing more, because nobody was pissed yet. We eventually left with no more than a few glances and the odd hand gesture being made to the other group. Being sober, I was observing events from a totally new perspective. I realised how explosive moments like that could be; the switch could flick at any time, with devastating consequences.

We called at a few more pubs and by one in the morning, I had heard enough banter for one night. The singing was getting louder and the behaviour more and more threatening, as it always did. I had had my fill for the night. This time I actually listened to the little voice that had whispered in my ear so many times in the past, telling me it was time to go home. Drink had always had the final say before but because I had been on soft drinks I was the master of my own destiny. I said my goodbyes to the predictable light-hearted chorus of 'yeah, fuck off', 'lightweight' and 'does the missus want you home, then?'

It felt good to leave and not feel like I was missing something. I went back to Paula's sister's house in Ivy Bridge where we were staying.

The following day I woke, and, while having breakfast, the front door alarm went and three police officers asked if I was present. Paula invited them in and after they had asked me a couple of questions and I had got dressed, I was taken to Charles Cross police station where I was questioned about an incident in the early hours of the morning. It quickly became obvious I hadn't been in Union Street when the offence took place. For the first time in my life I hadn't been wondering what shit I was in as we drove to the station because I knew that I hadn't done a thing. Nevertheless I was curious to find out what had happened, because I got the distinct impression it was serious.

I was right.

At half past three, Ian and the crew had again bumped into the Stonehouse lads we had seen in the Maritime and this time, with both sides tanked up and looking trouble, it had gone off. And gone off big time. During the fight, Ian threw a punch that apparently knocked David Taylor off his feet and as he fell he banged the base of his skull on the pavement. Taylor was seriously ill in hospital on a life-support machine but he deteriorated very quickly. A day later, his machine was turned off.

Over the years, the violence that my friends and I experienced in Plymouth was often ferocious. I had been in trouble from the age of ten, yet apart from the incident in Union Street, during which I took a severe beating, nobody was ever badly hurt. I have a few scars, no teeth and my right hand and the associated knuckles are a mess. There was the odd broken bone, too, stitching, bruising, burst noses and split lips but nothing more. Yet one punch from my brother and a young man had lost his life. Ian was placed on remand and charged with murder, which was later reduced to manslaughter. I visited him in Brixham prison and to see Ian a broken man made me glad I had turned my back on the life I had been leading. That could easily have been me in the jail cell. After a two-week trial in the Crown Court, he was sentenced to five years in prison, reduced to three on appeal.

If I had been present, no doubt I would have got involved in the brawl, and who knows what would have happened? But the guardian angel I believe we all have told me to get out. Sober, you can make the right decision. Drunk, no fucking chance. Wild horses wouldn't have dragged me away if I had been drinking so my efforts over the past eighteen months had been rewarded, if you can call it that.

There isn't a day that goes by that Ian doesn't regret what happened, but he can't turn back the clock and he served his time in prison. While one brother was incarcerated, my youngest brother Cathel was in a prison of his own making. I had booked a holiday for Paula and me and we took Arron, Charley and Brooke back to Plymouth to stay with their grandparents. Before we flew out, I arranged to meet Cathel while I had the chance, just to catch up and check on his progress. He was a quiet, gentle, unassuming person and while my teenage years had been consumed by alcohol, I had always given drugs a wide berth. By contrast many of Cathel's friends experimented with cannabis and other social drugs before progressing to the most devastating of them all, heroin.

Not everyone who drinks becomes an alcoholic and not everyone who takes drugs becomes an addict, but some people are genetically inclined to suffer from addiction, the drug of 'more'. If one feels good, then surely two will feel even better. Cathel had been to rehab centres on a couple of occasions and managed to get himself clean and I encouraged him to attend Narcotics Anonymous meetings because of the effect AA had had on my life. The problem was that his periods of recovery would vary before the vicious circle would begin again. It began with drink, followed by more drink, social drugs and eventually back on to heroin. For someone like me, suffering from a chronic addiction, total abstinence is the only way and I have always steered clear of mind-altering substances.

I met Cathel for lunch in Ivy Bridge and it was obvious he was on a downward spiral. He had been drinking and he admitted doing recreational drugs, but swore that he hadn't been doing heroin and I believed him. As his brother, I wanted to get him in a headlock and squeeze him into submission. I so wanted to reach him with words of wisdom that would stop this catastrophic cycle. The fact was I had done the threats on many previous occasions, but with no discernible effect. My parents had pleaded with him to get off it, get straight and stay clean but nothing worked. The thing that hurt more than anything was that he was my little brother and there was nothing I could do. It didn't matter that I could handle myself or that I was a professional footballer because none of it could help him.

'Cathel, you have to stop now. It will only get worse. You know the pattern. It is heroin next, then hospital and rehab. If you're lucky.'

You don't see old heroin addicts. They either get clean or they die. His eyes filled up and he nodded his head. We Morrisons don't do hugs, but I put my hand on his shoulder and ruffled his hair, saying, 'Come on mate, let's get out of here.'

We walked over to my car. I got in and Cathel stood by the window.

'Any chance of a sub, Andrew?' he asked.

'Go on, how much?'

'Just £20.'

'No chance,' I laughed.

He smiled, rolled his eyes, nodded and started to walk away. I drove up behind him, wound the window down and shouted to him.

'Here,' I said, handing him a tenner. As he took it his eyes filled up and tears ran down his cheeks.

'I'm gonna get myself sorted this time, Andy. I promise.'

'Make sure you do, mate. I'll see you soon.'

As he walked away, I remembered something he used to say as a kid. 'Ian beats you up Andrew; you beat Graham up; Graham beats me up. Who do I beat up? It's just so unfair.'

Life isn't fair.

I never saw Cathel alive again.

Paula and I flew out to Tenerife and I put my phone on charge with the intention of picking up my calls in a day or so. I wanted to relax and enjoy a bit of quality time with my wife. We enjoyed the hotel facilities, caught a bit of sun and after a long but enjoyable day, we went to sleep on our first night. Then, at six in the morning, the phone in our room rang. I took a few minutes to come around but finally I lifted the receiver to hear a Spanish voice telling me he was transferring a call. Then my dad's voice came on the line. 'Andrew. Where have you been? We've been trying to get hold of you all night.'

Before he could say anything, I blurted out, 'It's Cathel, isn't it Dad?'

There was silence for a few seconds. My dad's voice was choked. He could hardly speak.

'Yeah. He's gone, they found him this morning.'

I told him I was heading home and then told Paula. It had happened the previous night and Dad said he had to trace our hotel because they hadn't been able to get me on my mobile. I turned the phone on and had about ten missed calls and six messages. My stomach churned as I started to play my voicemails.

'I need to speak to you, please answer the phone,' Cathel pleaded.

Then I played the next message. It was Cathel again.

'Can you call me back as quickly as you can Andrew? I need to speak to you.'

So I've just learned that my kid brother is dead, yet I'm listening to him on my phone, begging for help. It was hard to get my head around. I don't know if I could have helped him or what he wanted to talk to me about. I never will. But after those calls he evidently went to see his dealer, got the gear he wanted and then died alone at a bus stop in Plymouth city centre in the early hours of the morning, alone. All his major organs had packed up and he died of a massive heart attack caused by a heroin overdose. He left behind a wife and an eighteen-month-old daughter.

We flew home, attended the inquest and he was buried in Plymouth shortly thereafter. They say time is a great healer, but I think you visit painful passages of your life less as time goes on because, when I think back, it hurts just as much as it did when I first found out. How does anyone get over losing their little brother?

What else could life chuck at me? Ian in prison, Cathel dead. I was numb but expected more shit to come my way at any moment, and I was right. It had been no more than a few weeks since Paula had gone to have a mole removed at our doctor's practice in Northwich. She hadn't been happy with this mole for some time but the doctor made it clear that the procedure wasn't done willy-nilly. Nevertheless they agreed to take this one off and to send it away for tests. Having heard nothing for a few weeks, she went back to see if the results were ready. Apparently, they had been lost so a call was made to the lab and Paula was told she would be contacted in due course.

She received a call the following day asking her to go to the surgery. The doctor told her she had a malignant melanoma in its harshest form. She called me and I went down to the surgery straightaway and the doctor told us he wasn't going to pretend it wasn't serious. She would need surgery on her shin and immediately, too.

A week later Paula had an area the size of an apple taken away from her leg, leaving what looked like a shark bite. Thankfully, however, the operation was a success as they managed to prevent the cancerous area from spreading any further. If she had not had the gumption to ask about the results, it would have been too late. For once, thank God, there was a happy ending. How I didn't turn back to drink during those horrendous few months is anyone's guess, but it convinced me that if I could come through those ordeals in one piece, I would be able to cope with anything.

That theory was going to be put to the test.

19

A Slug in the Guts

Andy Preece had probably been my best mate in football stretching back to my time at Blackpool and our wives have always got on really well, too, so we're pretty tight. He knew I had finished at City and as player-manager of Bury, he felt he could help me keep ticking over. He rang me and told me he had a great physio at Gigg Lane called Lee Nobes, who would help me get fit.

Andy thought it would be good for me and good for the club if I trained with Bury while working with Lee. It seemed like the ideal solution and the next logical step. I spent the remaining months of the 2001/02 season at Gigg Lane and Lee was fantastic, every bit as good as Andy had said (he would later become first-team physio at Manchester City). I had a break during the summer and then returned for pre-season 2002/03.

After a month or so back, I went to see my surgeon, Dai Reece, at Crewe and told him I was still struggling to get anywhere near the fitness levels I needed to be at. He did another exploratory op to see what was going on and he decided to adjust the ilia tibia band that runs from the knee to the hip because he felt it was too tight. He cut it and stretched it and then sewed it back in, but this was my final attempt at finding a surgical solution. I went back to Bury until Christmas, not feeling any real difference from where I'd been at previously. I called in to see Dai, who decided to have another look to see if there had been any had improvement. There hadn't.

'Whichever way you want to hear it, Andy, nothing has changed. You're not going to be able to play again,' Dai told me. It wasn't what I wanted to hear, but it was maybe what I needed to hear. I could finally move on.

I was thirty-two and that was it. I had not only missed the best part of four years through injuries but also lost the chance to pen the biggest contract of my career. In addition, all the chances to adapt and to move steadily towards coaching, as well as the opportunity to get my foot in the door at City with a half-pay and reserve-team-coach-type deal, had disappeared. I had missed out on everything, but I was at least fortunate that my best mate was in charge at Bury. We were like brothers in many ways. We would fight and argue from time to time but had a great rapport and enjoyed each other's company and so I was grateful when he let me take the reserves on a non-payment basis with a view to taking sessions with the defenders when I had picked up a bit of experience. It was a real eye-opener. These were my first steps into coaching and while I was keen to share my experience with some of the young talent at the club, it was all new. We had Michael Nelson and Danny Swales coming through so I was looking forward to the new role, but I had to learn on the job. It was unpaid and expenses only, but that suited me down to the ground.

Despite what my doc had advised I still felt I could get back playing. Financially, we needed something quickly because Paula and I had carried on living the footballer lifestyle, thinking there would be something on the horizon as a player. I needed a reality check because we were broke. It was essential to make the coaching work and so I threw myself into the role at Bury.

The problem was that the first time I was introduced to the lads as one of the Bury coaches I found it daunting. You think you know the game inside out and how things work, but it isn't until you're on the other side and the players are looking to you for words of inspiration that you realise you actually know nothing! Outside of my comfort zone I was completely tongue-tied.

Andy named the team to face Shrewsbury and then turned to me and said, 'This is Jock. He's going to be taking the reserves from now on. Over to you, mate.' He just fell silent. It was cue Andy Morrison. I can remember it like it was yesterday because the stage fright was overwhelming. There were twenty lads looking at me, waiting for me to speak. I had been put on the spot and I found it incredibly intimidating. As I had nothing planned I just babbled some rubbish about going out and doing their jobs right. I'm not sure what the players made of it, or of me. I made sure I had notes to refer to the next time I was given the chance to give a pep talk and things did improve. It was a challenge, but one that I needed to rise to or say goodbye to the game for good. I carried on working with the reserves and really enjoyed it. We had David Nugent coming through from the academy and I loved working on different aspects of defending with the lads during the week.

I officially retired as a professional footballer at Christmas 2002. I had delayed the inevitable for long enough and if I wanted to qualify for my FA pension – or rather cash it in early – I had to finish as a player.

I had at least made a start to my coaching career and Preecey was doing well as player-manager with the first team. A 0–0 draw with Wrexham on the final day of the season meant we just squeezed into the third-division playoffs in seventh spot. We would be playing Bournemouth over two legs, a side we had already beaten 2–1 home and away that season, so confidence was high. However, they held us to a 0–0 draw at Gigg Lane and then beat us 3–1 at Dean Court so the chance was gone. At least the board realised Preecey had done a good job and retained him for the following season.

It wasn't to last.

A few months later, and just halfway through the 2003/04 campaign, Preecey left Gigg Lane. With the team comfortably placed in mid-table, he was released as part of a cost-cutting exercise following a 4–0 defeat to Oxford United. It wasn't a case of the board feeling he wasn't up to the task; more a change in direction they felt would benefit everyone. Well, everyone except me and Andy!

Preecey was soon snapped up as a player by Carlisle while Graham Barrow was placed in temporary control at Bury. He asked if I would help him out so I was technically his number two, which I was a little uncomfortable with, but I went along with it initially. One of our first games was against Carlisle, which meant Preecey coming back to Gigg Lane just days after leaving. It's funny how often football seems to throw up these scenarios and I'd been speaking to him regularly so I knew he was pumped up for that game. He is the type of person who always rises to the occasion when he feels he has something to prove and he wanted to show the Bury hierarchy they had been wrong to show him the door. I've said to him many times that the problem comes when he is in the comfort zone. That's when he slips back. Put him in a corner and you will see what he's made of.

That said we went 1–0 up early on through Gareth Seddon but Preecey started to run things after that and he was easily the best player on the park, as they went on to win 3–1. He didn't celebrate any of the Carlisle goals, which, as I told him in no uncertain terms, is bollocks. I've always believed players not celebrating against their old teams is utter bullshit because it shows a lack of respect for your new team. I think it's more about egos and how you will be perceived by the fans. Knowing Preecey, he would have been doing cartwheels afterwards but he didn't want to show that on the day. Each to their own, I suppose.

I carried on alongside Graham until we were beaten 2–1 by Lincoln City and I suggested to him that maybe he needed someone with a bit more experience even though, looking back, I had more than enough experience to take the position on. Self-doubt and low esteem were still holding me back but I had made my mind up that it was time to move on. Whichever way you painted it, my heart just wasn't in it with Preecey gone. I had thought that maybe I'd be asked to stay on with the reserves, but it didn't work out that way and I left the club, fully expecting Preecey to get another job in management that would hopefully lead to us resuming our working relationship. But as he was still playing, there was nothing on the horizon and I was back to square one without a pot to piss in.

I could not have been more skint at the time. I was guilty of burying my head in the sand and not having the courage to look at the reality that, in football terms, I was no use to anyone. We had £4,000 a month leaving our account before living expenses and I felt that I was entitled to something, somewhere. I had worked since the age of sixteen and paid hundreds of thousands of pounds in taxes and now I had nothing. In the short term, my only option was to sign on. I went to the local job centre and was awarded jobseeker's allowance, which at least meant we'd have our council tax paid. People will no doubt think, 'why not get a job – any job?' I would have done anything, but I felt so fucking useless at the time and desperately wanted to stay in the game.

I had kidded myself for too long that I would find my way back to playing again. It was time to face reality. I went into the job centre with a baseball cap pulled low over my head in case anyone recognised me. I had neither qualifications nor a trade behind me. Fuck all. My career had ended so quickly but there was one thing I could still do. I contacted the PFA and discovered that I was able to take my non-contributory pension early because I had retired from football. They arranged for me to receive the lot: £54,000. It would free up the noose a little because I owed my father £16,000 and had a further £25,000 earmarked to clear credit cards and other debts. I also had a Barclays Select account, which made £25,000 available in funds but we were up to our limit with it, so I deposited the £54,000 into our main account while I worked out who needed paying first and what the breakdown would be.

I was supposed to inform the dole office of any change in circumstances, which I still hadn't done. I paid my dad and kept £38,000 in my account so I could continue to pay the minimum payments on my credit cards, loan and overdraft as well as having a bit of breathing space. That meant I had money showing in my account, which, of course was all spoken for, but it alerted the authorities to the fact that I had money I hadn't disclosed.

Unbeknown to me, my prosecution for fraud had begun.

Finally, in February 2005, more than a year after my last job in football, Preecey called and asked if I would mind going to watch Worcester City take on Hinckley in the Blue Square Premier League. He had been approached to take over as Worcester's manager and would be looking to take me with him as number two. Before making a final decision on the job he wanted my opinion on their setup so I headed to the Midlands in high spirits to see what they were all about. The two-hour drive wasn't so bad and the ground, though dated, had a great atmosphere. The team were struggling, but there were some really good players and a decent following of around eight hundred fans. It was a big city with lots of potential. I saw it as a great opportunity with investment promised and the possibility of a new stadium to boot.

I called Preecey after the game. 'Yeah, why not? Looks good and I think we should do it.'

In a matter of days we were installed and we started with a hard-fought draw a few days later. After that we kicked on, missing the playoffs by just a few points. It was great to be involved again and we quickly drew up plans for the new season, which would be our big push for promotion. We kept all the players we wanted and pushed the boat out to keep our best player, Adam Webster, who could easily have played at a much higher level. The problem for a lot of lads in non-league football is that they earn more in their day jobs than they could as a full-time professional. Webby earned £600 per week with us and was far and away our highest-paid player and he probably earned as much again from his job as an accountant. It wouldn't make sense for him to go to a club in the third or fourth division and get a one-year contract on £500 per week. Once you're in the job trap, it limits your ambition, even though I think he could have made a real go of it.

As Preecey and I planned Worcester's future, my own was hanging by a thread. The authorities were closing in. A letter arrived advising me to go down to the job centre, where I was interviewed under caution and told I had not informed them about my change in circumstances. I was charged with four counts of benefit fraud over a period from August 2003 to July 2005 and advised to get a solicitor. I hadn't even realised our council tax was still being paid or that any other benefits were forthcoming because I always left financial matters to Paula. I knew I was still receiving jobseeker's allowance, but that was it. Call it ignorance, or anything you like, but even if there had only been £5,000 in my account I would still have been liable for prosecution. In fact I had a lot more than that, though it was no more than a survival fund, aimed at keeping a roof over our heads until things improved.

My solicitor told me I should contest the charges because I had mitigating circumstances, but I was also warned that, if found guilty, I would get the book thrown at me. I didn't have it in me to go through a trial and I obviously didn't want it made public. I was skint and I was in the shit and I believed it would be a quick court case that would slip under the radar because I had been out of the public eye for a few years. Given what happened to me in court I should have contested the charges instead of deciding to plead guilty on all counts. For once I didn't stand up and fight an injustice. It was the wrong decision. The problem was that all my courage had evaporated. I didn't have the belly for another fight. My pride stopped me from allowing my financial situation to be exposed for all and sundry to see so I went to court hoping to get the matter sorted quickly and quietly, only to be met by the press before I had even got inside. My sentence was fifty hours of community service, which was the minimum penalty I could be given thanks to a judge who understood that this was a catalogue of errors on my behalf rather than anything devious. It had been put on record that I was naïve when it came to finances, which to some extent was true.

Throughout my career I had earned money, it was paid into the bank and that was that. The £54,000 had never really been mine. It was just to keep the family fed and the debtors at bay, but it had created nothing but problems. In fact, because the money was from my pension pot it could have stayed frozen until I was sixty-five. If I had just left there it wouldn't have had had any effect on my claim for income support. Now I was going to have to live with the stigma for the rest of my life and to compound matters the papers went to town on the story. I've been ridiculed by people ever since and for a man who has taken pride his whole life in being honest and giving 100 per cent, this was a slug in the guts. I was labelled a benefit cheat and there was nothing I could do about it. It's a scar that won't heal and there's not a day that goes by that I wish I hadn't fought those accusations. It's been tough and some people have made judgements about me based on what happened in court that day. They think all footballers are multi-millionaires and we're all bracketed together, despite the cavernous gap in what I earned alongside someone like Alfie Haaland. But there you go. That's life.

I did my community service of fifty hours with three lovely ladies in a Barnardo's store in Winsford, ironing shirts on a Saturday afternoon for a few weeks and paid my debt to society. If only certain members of society would have left it there, I would have been fine.

And so would they.

20

Another Demon Put to Bed

The people I knew and trusted had stood by me throughout the benefits ordeal and it's nice to be able to tell my side of the story without the sensational headlines. There's an advert for Carling out at the time of writing with the tag line, 'You know who your friends are.' How true that is. People who care about you are there when you need them while others, by contrast, are conspicuous by their absence.

At Worcester, we made pre-season as professional as possible, drawing on our long experience in the game. The lads loved it, saying it was the best they had ever known. In addition we changed our tactics and style of play, so that we'd get Webby on the ball at every opportunity. He would then, in turn, link play and express himself more. It also meant that we would be getting full value for money for his £600 per week. Were we putting all our eggs in one basket? In some ways, yes, but if it came off he would inspire us to promotion.

Things went really well – better in fact than we could have hoped for – and our first three pre-season games gave us every cause to feel quietly confident about the season ahead. However, our last friendly, against Kidderminster Harriers at home, was about to change everything and for me it was another black mark on my CV.

The game was a local derby but not a bitter one; that was saved for Worcester–Hereford clashes. It was a beautiful July day with a good crowd turning up and a last chance to fine tune before the big kickoff the following weekend. I had never heard of Mark Yates, the Kidderminster manager, as either a player or anything else, but I found him to be obnoxious from the moment I clapped eyes on him. In short, he came over as an arrogant cunt, strutting around as if he was Jose Mourinho. I said nothing at the time. I'd moved on, hadn't I? I mentioned to our chairman that the guy looked a bit of a prick and he agreed: Yates, he told me, was well known for thinking he was something special; the best thing to do was ignore him. 'He's never achieved fuck all,' the chairman added for good measure.

I have fallen out with many players and managers during my career. It is impossible to get on with everyone you work with. But in my book, if ever anyone was in need of a slap, it was Yates. There was just something about him that got my fucking back up.

The game kicked off and, two minutes in, Webby received a pass and took the ball on the outside of his right foot before playing it off. Then, after what seemed like three seconds later, their six-foot-five centre half, Mark Creighton, who was known as 'Killer' by the Kidderminster fans, dived in with a tackle and snapped Webby's left leg. His tendons, ligaments and bone all went, but because the tackle had been so late, nobody saw it. The referee had turned away and most of the fans had followed the ball. I, however, saw everything.

In my view, it wasn't so much a tackle more a cowardly assault, the sort you make when you are looking to take revenge on another player for something he did to you. Except Webby didn't know Creighton and had no history with him. Anyone with knowledge of the game knew how bad the challenge had been and while the likes of Aaron Ramsey and Eduardo of Arsenal have been badly hurt by clumsy, badly timed challenges in recent times, this, to my way of thinking, went well beyond that. Webby was stretchered off and taken to hospital in tears. There wasn't a single word of apology or even a slight show of concern from their bench. I stood on the touch-line, taking everything in, totally numb. I would like to say that I was concerned for Webby and worried about whether he would ever play again, but if I'm honest, I wasn't thinking any of those things. All the old demons were circling around my head. I felt my instincts challenging me to act on what I had just witnessed.

'Six-foot-five-inch Killer. You gonna let him get away with that, are you? Do something about it. All the players will know you've shit it if you don't do something about it.'

That is what I was telling myself.

Their fans were shouting 'Killer, Killer,' and there he was, running around the pitch, crunching into one tackle after another. I had no defence against my feelings and it was pointless even trying. There was only one course of action available. But I was no longer a kid fuelled by alcohol. I was assistant manager of Worcester City and should have been past that kind of behaviour. If I did react, the repercussions would be grave. But as I tried to reason with myself, I heard a voice say: 'You can't go there anymore, Andy. Those days are gone, just leave it.' That was countered with a more familiar argument. 'Fuck off you shithouse. Fucking coward – you just don't want it. He's too big for you.'

Suddenly, I'm back in that dark place again where there's no reasoning and nothing seems real. I had seen that movie so many times before, but there was no escaping. More worryingly, I'm not drunk. The only surprise was that I managed to hold myself in check for almost an hour.

On sixty-three minutes, Creighton went down with a calf strain and after the physio had checked him over, he signalled to the bench that he wanted to come off. He limped towards the touchline and headed straight for the changing rooms. I felt no adrenalin, no rage. I got up and calmly walked down the side of the pitch. There was no arguing in my head anymore. I was well past that. A strange calmness had entered my soul.

I entered the changing room and walked over to Creighton.

'Right, try and break my fucking leg you cunt.'

He stood up, hands out and said, 'Come on, Andy. It was an accident.'

I smashed him on the side of the head and he fell back against the wall, cowering, covering his face with his hands. I grabbed his collar and dragged him up.

'I fucking knew you'd shit it. I fucking knew you had no bollocks, you big fucking pussy.'

I banged his head against the wall and started to walk out, at which point the Kidderminster captain raced in. He had been on the bench and must have been told to go and check everything was all right. He came towards me and I invited him to chance his arm, 'Do you fucking want some as well?' He ran behind the massage table and hid. I can't blame him because while I was there physically, I wasn't mentally, if that makes sense.

'Come on big un. It's not worth it.'

I turned and walked back along the touchline and as I passed their bench I winked at Yates.

'Killer my fucking arse. He's a fucking shithouse.'

He wouldn't have known what I was on about at that point so I carried on and stood alongside Preecey, who, without looking at me, asked, 'You haven't fucking hurt him, have you?'

By this time, their physio had been into the changing rooms, after which he sprinted back to the bench to tell Yates what had happened. Yates listened, looked over at us and then calmly walked on to the pitch and called his team off before leading them back down the tunnel, leaving the fans bemused. Their lads traipsed off while our players had their hands on their hips, wondering what the fuck was going on.

Oh, shit. What had I done?

I didn't know what options Yates had, but he later said what had happened wasn't in the spirit of the game. My view was that the tackle on Webby hadn't been either, not to mention the lack of an apology. To this day, neither Yates nor Creighton, or for that matter anyone at Kidderminster Harriers, have contacted us to see how Webby was. He eventually recovered, but he lost six months of his career thanks to that tackle.

I was charged by the FA, fined two weeks' wages by the club and suspended for three games. At my disciplinary hearing I pleaded guilty, was fined £750 and banned for a further six games. Did I regret it? No. Would I do it again? No. I would find another way of dealing with it but I wouldn't exact revenge in the same manner. I was given an informal dressing down by Worcester and reminded of my responsibilities and future conduct. Nevertheless, the chairman made it clear I had his full support and, to some extent, he understood why I had done what I had done. Sacking me was never an option. The players had written a letter to the club, making it clear that they would ask for a transfer if I was fired, but that was never needed. Webby was still in hospital at that point and the board needed to be seen to be doing the right thing. I appreciated the club's backing and the moral support from the lads. I would never have let them hand in that letter, but it proved we were together as a team. More so than ever.

We took that team spirit into the season and had a good year – despite being without Webby until December – and had a great run in the FA Cup, one that would see me come up against one of my former clubs along the way. We beat Accrington Stanley, who would go on to be promoted from the Conference that season, after holding them at their place. The next tie was with Chippenham, in the first round proper, and again we brought them back to our place after drawing away from home. The draw for the second round had taken place by the time the replay came round. There was tremendous pressure on us because we knew that the winners would face Huddersfield Town and that the game would be screened live on *Match of the Day*. With the carrot of a home tie against League Two opposition, plus £100,000 in television revenue, more than two thousand fans packed into our ground and Chippenham, who were a division below us, made us battle all the way. It was a horrible, scrappy game that we managed to edge 1–0 courtesy of Webby, who had just come back into the team after his long layoff.

The relief afterwards was tangible because that kind of windfall can set a club up for a good twelve months and we felt we'd done our bit in guaranteeing that. Sadly, we lost 1–0 to Huddersfield, who were no better than us on the day but we lacked a cutting edge and that was the end of that. We had our noses rubbed in the dirt when the draw was made straight after the match. All we could hear was their changing room going bananas. It turned out they had drawn Chelsea away. What a day out that would have been for our lads, but we'd had a great run and couldn't really complain.

We didn't win promotion but it had been an enjoyable first full season and I think that we probably underachieved overall. I was becoming a little frustrated at the level I was coaching at because I'd finished my A licence at Aberystwyth, where I had been on the same course as Paul Jewell, Gary Speed, Simon Grayson, Tommy Wright and Steve Davis and they have all gone on to do well in the game. The problem was that I had been used to better facilities and better players. Don't get me wrong, they were a cracking set of lads, but I'm not someone who can accept mediocrity and the fact I had played in the Premier League alongside players like Alan Shearer, David Batty, Tim Sherwood and Ian Bishop and trained with people like George Weah was starting to grate, even if I was aware that I needed to walk before I could run.

Another problem was that I had been struggling to deal with the limitations of life on the sidelines. Although the condition of my knee meant that I couldn't play anymore, my heart was still on the pitch. I longed to be competing, tackling, heading, shouting, organising and intimidating. It was what I'd done from the age of ten and it was all I knew. I missed the buzz, the atmosphere in the changing rooms and getting into the zone on match-days, when your mind, body and spirit are on a higher plane. Then there was the ninety minutes of solid action, followed by the gradual comedown in the hours and days after the game. It was a drug. Playing had been just as addictive as alcohol and just as hard to give up. I couldn't replace that experience and I would sometimes sit for hours in the changing room after everyone had gone home, unable to handle the fact I could no longer play. I felt utterly lost. I was also chronically depressed and continually had vivid dreams of being on trial at a club and telling Paula we would be fine because there was a new deal on the table and our money worries would soon be over.

I was suffering from a bad case of self-pity, that most unattractive of emotions. There was so much more happening in the world: people dying; wars; nations starving to death; all of it so much more serious than my little predicament. I had so many things to be grateful for: my family, my health, my friends and a new direction as a coach. I tried positive self-talk, but the reality was I felt I had fuck all to offer anyone.

I am not the type to turn up, take the money and hang around. Preecey, however, said we should stay put and give it another go, because it would be harder to find another club being out of the game. I wasn't convinced. The thing is, not every club has the ambition necessary to move through the leagues. Promotion brings its own problems in bigger wage bills, ground improvements and greater expectations. Some clubs are happy to stay in their own little comfort zone and don't want to rock the boat. Those clubs don't want people coming in and telling them that they need to change this or that if they want to go progress. They want to go to places like Redditch with their club blazers on, have a drink in the clubhouse after the match and then say, 'Thanks, gents. See you next season.'

In hindsight, I should have walked away that summer, but I stayed and grew steadily more frustrated. Such was my mood that it didn't take much to push me over the edge. About three games into what would be my final season at Worcester we were away to Kettering Town and there was a guy by the dugout giving us all dogs' abuse. I glanced over to see who it was. He looked like your typical gobshite so I ignored him. But he carried on, singling me out for the treatment. The funny thing is, if you've got thirty thousand people chanting abuse in your direction, calling you a fat bastard or whatever, you don't hear it and it means nothing. When it's just one voice and you can see where it's coming from, it suddenly becomes highly personal because you not only hear every word, but also see the hate on their face and the intent in their eyes. That's when you think about sorting the problem out.

It began as general banter; then he crossed the line a couple of times. At first I tried to rise above it and blanked it out of my mind. A month later, due to the way the fixtures fell, we played Kettering again. The same bloke had obviously done a little research on me and my chequered past on the internet. As I went out to take the warm-up before the game, he was in our paddock with a few of his mates. This time he was really going for it.

Our chairman, Dave Boddy, came over to me because by this time it was getting embarrassing. He said that he'd have them thrown out, but I told him to let it go. Fair play to him Dave went over and asked my tormentors to pack it in but it didn't do any good. As the match began, this guy, thickset and about my age, started up again. It got so bad that the other lads in the dugout couldn't look me in the eye.

'You fat fucking thug, are you going down the Job Centre in the morning? You fucking cheating cunt. You're scum Morrison.' He was shouting things I was actually thinking about myself. My son was in the crowd and there was deathly silence. I felt that the focus of everyone in the stadium was on me and I wished the ground would open up and swallow me whole.

By the end of the game, I was at the end of my tether and turned to face the crowd behind us. I invited Big Mouth down to the touchline to continue his comments. He tried to get through the stewards who had been sent to stand around him but they, along with his mates, held him back. He put his finger across his throat, indicating that mine was going to get cut and then, among other threats, he said that he was going to rip my head off. I told the stewards to let him through, it was fine by me, but they wouldn't.

Eventually he was taken out and that was the end of that. At least for the time being. We weren't scheduled to play them again that season and I tried to put it out of my mind but, as ever, it ate away at me. I remembered what he had said and the fans around him laughing their heads off; I could see the embarrassment of the lads around me and then see his face, contorted with hate as he targeted me. It was an unusual situation, something that I had never encountered before. I felt physically sick that I had let the rage consume me in a way that would only end when I dealt with it. I couldn't get it out of my head. Call me weak, call me immature, but he had got inside my head despite my best efforts. It didn't matter who I talked to or what they said, my mind was made up. That fucker would have to back up his words. And sooner rather than later.

I knew what the solution was. Kettering's next game was at Redditch, who we would be playing before long, so I told Preecey I was going to scout the game. He had a big smile on his face.

'You're not going to fucking get involved are you?'

'Don't be silly,' I replied.

I said I was going to run my eye over Redditch and that was it. The next day I drove to their ground feeling totally calm. I hadn't a clue whether this guy would be there or not. If he was, we would see what happened; if not, it was no big deal. Being a local derby Kettering had taken about five hundred fans to the game and as I sat in the stand I occasionally looked at the away end. I didn't spot him until about five minutes before half-time, when I saw a bloke walk down to the front of the terracing. My heart started pumping. 'That's fucking him,' I thought. It was payback time, time to quieten those questioning voices in my head.

My mind made up I got up and walked behind the stand, where I caught sight of him going into the toilets. I had a woolly hat and scarf on and I followed him into the toilets, which were empty.

A door opened. Big Mouth stepped out of a cubicle and went over to wash his hands. He didn't notice me, so I walked up and tapped him on the shoulder.

'All right, mate?'

He turned around and said, 'Yeah, great.' He looked at me, trying to work out who I was. I took my hat and scarf off. He looked at me again and it must have sunk in, because the blood drained out of his face.

'Oh yeah, it's, erm . . . Andy Morrison from Worcester, isn't it?'

'Yeah, that's right,' I smiled. 'So, are you going to rip my fucking head off, then?'

'What do you mean?'

I grabbed him around the windpipe, my finger and thumb touching and lifted him up against the wall.

'I'm gonna let you go, and this is your chance. You're gonna rip my head off, you're gonna rip my eyes out and you're gonna fucking kill me and hurt my family. Is that right, you cunt? That's what you shouted the other week, wasn't it? Well, when I let you go, that's your chance.'

As I held him, I looked down and I could see that he had pissed himself. I released my grip and he slid down the wall.

'What are you doing? You tried to fucking kill me,' he spluttered, catching his breath.

'I knew you'd be a fucking coward. I fucking knew it. But I had to make sure.'

I could have asked a hundred managers and a hundred players and they would all have said the same thing. He's a shithouse, just leave him. Rise above it. And I should have done. But it had been such a personal attack that I couldn't. He got up, brushed himself off and started to walk out. He looked back.

'You're supposed to be a professional. You're not supposed to do this sort of thing.'

Then he left. All I could think of was the guy who had been held back in the stands at our place. He was a wild animal, desperate to get at me. It may have been an act, but if it was, he was playing the part well. All that talk, all those threats, all that bravado. Yet he had pissed his pants.

He went back to the lads he was with and I sat back down in the stand. I wondered whether he'd go and fetch twenty of his mates and come looking for me. I didn't need that, I had done what I came to do. The best thing now was to leave quietly. I walked out to my car and drove home. When I arrived I texted my dad, with whom I had discussed the matter during the week: 'Another demon put to bed.' I felt great but, as I came out of the adrenalin rush and reality kicked in, I knew what a risk I'd taken. But it didn't matter. Even if it had gone wrong I would rather have spent ten years in jail for really hurting him, rather than living with the suppressed rage. I know that sounds extreme, but it's how I felt. The boil had to be lanced. Now I could move on and I also had chapter and verse on Redditch's set plays and team formation as a bonus!

I saw Preecey back at our ground the next day and he asked how it had gone. 'Good, I think we'll enjoy playing them. They don't look much.'

'You didn't, did you?'

'Nah, not really. I just had a quiet word.'

We both hoped that would be the end of it but the fuckwits seemed to be on a factory production line and I allowed myself to rise to the bait with another gobby fan a few weeks later. We were playing Redditch away and a few things were shouted down from the stands during the game, most of them directed at me. Afterwards, we all went into their club bar for a few drinks and I was stood among our lads when I spotted one of the guys who had been shouting at me at the other end of the bar. He was looking straight at me, uneasily, probably wondering if it might be a good idea to leave. I asked him, 'Why stand on the terraces shouting all that shit? I'm here now. Why don't you abuse me now? Better still, why don't we go out into the car park and you shout the same things at me?'

I left it at that because, like all his type, he couldn't back up his threats. I went home and thought no more about it, but he took it a step further. Encouraged by one of our own directors, he wrote to the club complaining about me, adding that I had asked him to step outside for a straightener. It was a point in the season where we were out of the cups and not in with a chance of going up and the board were obviously thinking about a change of management. For those reasons I wasn't surprised when they informed me they were looking into the matter. I was however disappointed they had decided not to back me, which is too often the case in football. Little did I know they had been setting me up all along.

Earlier in my career, when I was a valuable asset as a player, my misdemeanours were overlooked; sacking me would have been to the detriment of the club. But if they are looking to get rid of you and you give them the opportunity, your feet won't touch the ground.

The following week we played Barrow at home and won 3–0. Afterwards, as usual, I went into the director's box for a Coke. While I was at the bar, I was handed a letter telling me that the board had convened a meeting to discuss the incident and to determine if action needed to be taken. The directors were all present when I read it and I couldn't believe they were taking it this far.

My reaction was typically forthright. 'Are you fucking sure? You fuckers are stitching me up, you fucking sneaky bastards. This is fucking bollocks and you know it. Why don't you show some balls? You don't even know who this fan is or what he did.'

I uttered a few more insults, screwed up the letter, threw it on the floor and went home. The meeting had been scheduled for Monday so I turned up on time for what I assumed was a disciplinary and sat down with the chairman and six directors. The chairman opened the proceedings.

'You're correct in what you said about the Redditch fan and if we did this every time somebody wrote in with a complaint, there would be about twenty enquiries a season. We accept that, but your behaviour in the director's box on Friday night, where you called the directors a bunch of wankers and backstabbing two-faced cunts, was unacceptable. We feel it would be in the best interests of the club if you moved on.'

I allowed myself a smile and thought, 'well done'. They had done me like a kipper and there was no going back. I walked right into their trap and had only myself to blame. The chairman put the obligatory statement in the local paper, praising my contribution to the club. There was no compensation: I was only on expenses and had no contract, while Preecey was on a bloody good contract. It was easy to set me up and get rid because it cost them nothing, but it wasn't that long before Preecey left, too. They had been desperate to get rid of him but had to wait until a bad run of results part way into the next season before they had justification. I should have followed my gut instinct and walked in the summer, but there you go. I put it down to experience and I learned a lot from that episode. The good thing is that the cronies at Worcester – the chairman and the directors – have all gone now too. Just desserts, I call it.

So my Worcester adventure was at an end and if I was going to get back into the game I needed to develop myself further because there were still a lot of boxes unticked on my CV. I also realised that I needed to acquire skills that I could make a living from outside of football so I went to Glasgow for three months on a personal-training and sports-massage course. I could no longer rely on a steady income from the game and it was time to stop dreaming that a well-paid coaching role was going to fall into my lap. I had my licences but either because I never really put my name out there or circulated my CV – or more likely because of the reputation I had in the game – nobody was knocking on my door with an offer of work.

I was looking for direction, a break, or just a chance to get things moving again and was doing bits and bobs just to get by until I could get back into football. In truth, a lot depended on Preecey getting back into work because, without him, it was going to be difficult.

21

Doing a Cantona

I am no Tiger Woods, but I joined Hartford golf club and tried to improve my game as a gentle walk around the greens relaxed me and gave me time to think. I got to know a few of the lads at the club, including Steve Bond, a well-known, popular lad who played a lot of football in the local leagues around Northwich. Bondy's local was the Bowling Green and he told me he was going to be managing their pub team before long and would I go and play a few games for them? He said it would be a good laugh and it would be good to have me on board because he wanted to win the league in his first season in charge. In addition, half his team were City fans. I said I couldn't commit to anything long term because I was hoping to get back into the professional game. However, as I was doing nothing at that point, I told him that I would play when I could, subject to what my knee would allow. It turned out that I managed to play a bit more often than I had imagined and although the standard was what you would expect of Sunday League football, I enjoyed getting my boots on for a competitive game.

Of course, it was bound to lead to the odd altercation but even with my chequered past I could never have imagined that one spat would end with me in Crown Court and the threat of up to two years in prison hanging over my head. I got a phone call early one Sunday from Bondy, asking me if I could play against a pub team called Broadhurst, who hailed from Winsford. I was at a loose end, so I went along and played for him. There were a few things said during the game but none of their lads seemed to know me or commented that I was, for all intents and purposes, a ringer. We won 3–2 in what had been a blood-and-thunder encounter, with a header from me clinching it in the ninetieth minute. That was that and I went home. I played a few games in between but I generally needed a couple of weeks between each appearance because my knee would swell up and stiffen, with the result that I found it hard to walk for three or four days.

A couple of weeks later, the phone went again on Sunday morning. It was Bondy.

'We've got Broadhurst again. Come on Andy. We're desperate for you to play. I want to beat those fuckers.' He is a persuasive guy and he went on in a similar vein for another minute before I gave in. We were playing away at Moss Farm and I turned up in my kit and went straight onto the pitch, getting there seconds before kickoff. Everyone was ready to go and as I jogged to my position I got a torrent of abuse from the Broadhurst players, three of whom were particularly vocal.

'This is a pub league, mate. Not Maine Road.'

'Haven't you got anything better to do you big fat cunt?'

'Why don't you just fuck off?'

'They paying you for this? Yeah, you need the money don't you coz you haven't got a fuckin' job.'

A few of them had clearly cottoned on to who I was and had done a bit more research on me, too. It was clear that some of them were still pissed from the night before and a couple were just finishing cigarettes off on the touchline, but all eyes were on me, wondering how I'd react. Some people might wonder why I was there and why I bothered putting myself in a situation like that. But I can't give a rational explanation. It's just me and how I am. I did what I wanted, regardless of the consequences and, if I had to pay later, I would. My gut feeling was that I shouldn't be there, but I couldn't leave the lads on my team short and, as you've probably sussed by now, there was part of me that wanted to answer those mouthy twats. I just thought, 'fuck it' and got on with the game.

Fair play to Bondy, who went over to the fuckers who were giving it out and pointed out they should leave well enough alone because they were biting off more than they could chew. It fell on deaf ears and besides I was an ex-professional footballer and, as lads like that all know, we're all soft fuckers, aren't we? We won't react because we're conditioned to rise above it, so it's okay to have a go because they had bought their ticket, entitling them to say whatever the fuck they wanted. Yeah, well, not me.

Eric Cantona said that when he karate-kicked that Crystal Palace fan as he walked down the touchline after being sent off, he was doing it for every professional footballer in the country who had to put up with the same shit week in, week out. I can relate to that and I'm sure many others can too.

The difference now was that I wasn't getting paid to take that crap. Nor had my critics paid to get in, so the restrictions, in my mind, had been lifted. My three tormentors – all Manchester United fans – continued to give me shit throughout the game. There were threats of violence, the finger across the throat, the promise that I'd be 'getting a visit' because they knew where I lived. It was non-stop. I just yawned and carried on. Big fucking deal.

As the time ticked on, their captain invited me to meet him in the car park of the Winnington Arms, where they drank. He didn't need to bother. This was a party invitation I was going to write myself and I had every intention of attending. I later found out he had a history of violence, including the use of a baseball bat on someone who had crossed him. It wouldn't have made a blind bit of difference.

'You're all full of shit,' I told him. 'None of you have got the balls to back it up. Go on then, meet me in the car park afterwards. I'll see you up there and we can discuss it further.'

Before the end, their captain sealed his fate by bringing up Cathel as we waited for a corner to be taken.

'Your brother still doing the drugs? Is he off them yet?'

People have said at various points in my life that I'm a strong person, but I'm not. I'm as weak as piss because I knew that I was going to take the easy option rather than the hard one, which for me, would have been walking away; putting it down as sticks or stones. But I couldn't let them get away with abusing my family or with the other things they had said.

After the final whistle, I walked off the pitch without shaking hands with anyone and headed straight for the dressing room, where

I quickly got changed. As I was walking to my car, the three lads who'd given me shit throughout the game drove past giving me the wanker hand-sign, laughing as they went. They weren't kids. They were in their early thirties, just a few years younger than me.

As always, I didn't debate the issue with myself. There was no question of what was right or wrong. I was in the zone. The decision had been made and the adrenalin was pumping through my body. Someone was going to get hurt. I followed their car and I could see them looking back, knowing I was behind them. All the laughing and hand gestures had stopped.

They knew something momentous was about to go off.

Both cars drove into the Winnington Arms car park and the captain jumped out of the car out as I pulled in. He started jumping about, inviting me to try my luck. I got out and the other two jumped out of the car to egg him on.

'Fuckin' do him.'

'Fuckin' kill him, Pete.'

I walked towards them and looked at the other two as I approached.

'Keep out of it. You'll get your chance when I've finished with him.'

I kept walking forwards and as I approached the mouthy fucker, he smacked me twice. I didn't feel a thing and wasn't for stopping. I grabbed him, threw him against his car, slapped him a few times and then put one hand around his throat and choked him until he passed out. I invited the other two to take his place. They had quietened down by this point and I went up to a six-foot-four gangly piece of shit, someone who had been just as vocal during the game. His mate had bolted into the pub, leaving him to face the music alone.

'Come on Andy, we're all grownups,' he pleaded. 'This is stupid. There's no need for it.'

I grabbed him and said, 'Either fuck off or apologise.'

'I'm sorry, Andy,' he stammered. 'It was just banter. We wanted to wind you up.'

I said nothing, let him go and got back into my car and drove home. I would like to say that they felt embarrassed by the whole incident, having had their pants pulled down and meekly accepting it. As Bondy had warned them, they had bitten off more than they could chew and I hoped they had learned a valuable lesson and would put it behind them.

Silly me!

At five o'clock that afternoon the police arrived at our house and arrested me, taking me to Middlewich detention centre. I was put in a cell, where I stayed for nineteen hours. I was questioned at just gone noon the next day, after a long, long night. It turned out that the three 'warriors' from Broadhurst had made a complaint to the police, who charged me with actual bodily harm. The captain – who had challenged me, threatened me, invited me to meet him after the game and then punched me twice before I did a thing – had somehow become the victim. It proved what I had known all along: he was a shithouse who could give it out all day long, but when the chips were down, couldn't back up his big words. Now I was facing a prison sentence for doing nothing more than taking up his invitation.

The trial came around fairly quickly and was held at Chester Crown Court. This time, I am pleased to say, and unlike the benefit charge, I stuck to my guns and pleaded not guilty. I wanted a jury to determine if I was guilty or not. It was a gamble because all people had to do was Google my name and they would find out about my previous misdemeanours. In fact I think that's what happened, because the first jury couldn't make a decision: six were with me, six against. A new jury was sworn in and a retrial ordered. After the new trial was completed the jury pontificated for a while until the judge asked if they were in a position to make a decision. When they told him that was unlikely, he ruled that the prosecution had had enough chances to convince the jury and dismissed the case. Acquitted again. I believe justice prevailed and I couldn't thank my excellent defence team enough, two of whom, incidentally, were City fans. Jeremy, I owe you a drink!

I was relieved because the repercussions would have been very serious and could even have ended my career in football. But something quite serious was troubling me. When I got into trouble after a drinking session, it was because I couldn't help myself. What bothered me now was that I'd been sober when I took care of Creighton during the Kidderminster match; I'd been sober when I went looking for the Kettering fan; I'd been sober when I followed these three clowns back to their pub. I was accountable on all three occasions. I had a choice, but I carried on regardless. If I had been punished for all three of those incidents, I could have had no argument. It is an area I need to work on, for everyone's sake, but I am getting there.

In February 2009, I got a call from Preecey, who had been installed as Northwich Victoria's new boss, asking if I wanted to be his number two, and I was delighted to accept. Vics had been struggling and had spoken informally with him the previous October, but Steve King had got the job. King was from down south and had a reasonable reputation at non-league level, but, based on my own experience at Worcester, you can't commute at this level. You need to be on top of things. He had also brought in a few London-based lads and not only was it not working, it was also expensive. It ended with a mutual parting of the ways and the chairman Jim Rushe asked Preecey if he could take training on the day King left.

There was a good squad of players at Vics but there was a lot of negativity around the place because of what had gone on previously. The club had been in administration and had been locked out of its own ground, with the result that a couple of games were played at Altrincham. To make the upheaval even greater new owners had come in.

We had been brought in at short notice on the Tuesday morning and we had a game that night against, of all clubs, Kettering, which we drew 0–0. We were off and running. Funnily enough, I didn't see the guy who had pissed himself that day.

The lads were classed as full time but because of the financial situation, we only trained a couple of times a week. We were well adrift at the foot of the table and within a few matches we realised that the fitness levels were inadequate. We tried to pick everybody's spirit up, get the place feeling positive again and tried to implement some of our ideas in training. We had some success in the early stages, winning our last six games on the spin, with Preecey picking up the manager-of-the-month award for April, while one of the lads won the divisional player-of-the-month award. Had we been in since October, when Preecey had originally been interviewed, we would probably have kept the club up. Unfortunately, however, we ran out of time and were relegated to the Conference North.

   Six weeks from the end of that season, I received a call I'd been half-expecting from Willie Donachie. Willie had spoken to me a few months before, gauging whether I would be interested in a bit of coaching work with him further down the line. Now, he wanted me to go out to Antigua where he had been working for about eighteen months as director of football and help him get the Antigua national team in shape. The money wasn't great, but the opportunity was too good to miss. I spoke to Preecey and our chairman and went with their blessing, on the understanding I would be back for pre-season. Everything was tied up very quickly and by the second week of April, I was flying out to Antigua for three months with the possibility of even longer if things worked out. Willie had wanted me out there as quickly as possible as he was planning a return visit to the UK with representatives from the Antiguan FA. They planned to speak to a number of English clubs in the hope of establishing a formal link with the Barracudas, whose owners hoped it would become the first professional club on the island.

   It wasn't easy to leave Paula and the kids behind, but it was a great chance to learn from someone I had so much respect for. I would also get the experience of coaching a national team, albeit a minnow in the grand scheme of things. Working with all age groups, including under-16s and under-21s, it would be a good addition to my CV.

   After a nine-hour flight, I was picked up at the airport by a tanned, fit-looking Willie. What a job it turned out to be. We trained from half-past seven until nine each morning, and then from half-six until half-eight every evening. It was a six-week training camp in preparation for the Parbo Bier Cup in Surinam, a four-team tournament made up of the hosts, French Guyana, Guyana and Antigua.

   The conditions were exactly as Willie had described to me on the phone and I'm not exaggerating when I say that British health-and-safety laws would not allow the players even to train on the pitches. They were just so bad. There was no grass, just rock-hard, burnt ground with gravel, which was littered with stones, empty cans and rubbish. We spent the first four or five days just taking sharp or dangerous objects off the training pitch. This was Antigua and cricket took precedence over everything else so football had to make do with whatever it was given. We may have begun training at 6.30

a.m., but players would arrive any time up until 7.30, usually with the response, 'Chill coach. It's cool. It's only training, man.' It was cool for them, frustrating for me.

As the competitive games drew closer, the better players started turning up more often. George Dublin was a talented centre-half and our captain. He played in a pro league in Trinidad and was respected by the other players. His season had ended and when he returned home to Antigua we invited him along to training, which he agreed to do. The players seemed to become more punctual after that because they looked up to him.

Getting the Antigua players interested was no mean feat and it wouldn't be uncommon for us to drive around in a pickup truck, knocking on the doors of full internationals to ask if they were coming to training or not. At times I felt like John Candy in the movie *Cool Runnings*! My instinct was to say to them don't bother, but these were the best players on the island and pretty much all we had to work with. Everything was totally amateur and the players either worked or hung around their villages, chillin' as they would call it, during the day. There were three or four guys who could have played at a much higher level and would not have been out of place at Championship level in England.

There were, however, many positives. I loved the people of Antigua and I loved the culture. It was a fantastic life: training, beach and gym and the opportunity to work with Willie and pick his brain on tactics and training methods. The food was great and the weather hot, with blue skies every day. We usually ate after training back at our accommodation in Five Islands, a small village outside the main town of St John's, where the president of the Antiguan FA had a couple of flats beneath his house. It was basic, but ideal for what we needed, with shower, fridge and a bed. The food was cooked for us every day by the president's wife and she sorted all our meals, breakfast, lunch and dinner. Willie and I trained, rested and carried out daily spiritual practices, which included reading, CDs and meditation. It was all geared to becoming more aware of the mind, giving more attention to the moment and focusing on the task in hand.

While I was out there, I got a call from City, saying they were going to commemorate the tenth anniversary of the 1999 playoff final. I was asked if I would come out onto the pitch with a few of the other lads before the Bolton game. I replied that I was out in Antigua, but would love to come. I had been in the West Indies for seven weeks by then and it would be a good chance to see Paula and the kids, too. I flew home and met up with Paul Dickov, Tony Vaughan, Gareth Taylor and Gerard Wiekens at the City of Manchester stadium. Before kickoff, we waited in the tunnel for what would be the last game of the season. We were introduced to the 47,000 crowd and I was taken aback by the incredible reception I got. I gave the fans a wave and they were singing my name. In all honesty I was overwhelmed. It was a reminder of how great those fans had been with me and you could never tire of that kind of ovation. It's wonderful to know they hadn't forgotten that period in the club's history. I managed to get a DVD of that day and guess what? Not a sign of Clinton Morrison!

I stayed at home for a few more days and had some quality time with the family before returning to Antigua, where the tournament was due to take place in another week or so. Willie and I upped the training intensity before we flew out to Surinam via Barbados to take part in our first competitive matches since I arrived.

We played our opening game against French Guyana the day after arriving and enjoyed a 2–1 win, which was a great start, although we rode our luck. Surinam were the favourites and had flown in six full-time professionals who had dual nationality for the tournament, the best known of whom was Edgar Davids. They were expected to waltz home, but lost their first game against Guyana, who went on to win the cup. I had met some fantastic people and it was an unforgettable experience. A win, a draw and a defeat, not bad, but, more importantly, the players had bought into my ideas on set plays and defending as a unit.

We flew back and continued training with the under-21s, who had a friendly against Grenada on the horizon. When the time came to travel, one of our best players, Ramji, didn't turn up for the plane, claiming to be unwell and not able to travel. We left without him, played the game and returned on the Monday. As I passed through the arrivals hall, I saw a picture of Ramji on the back of the *Antigua Sun*. He was being held aloft by his teammates after scoring the winning goal for his village team, which had beaten its bitter rivals. The truth was that in many ways playing for your village team was more rewarding than playing for the national team. They didn't get paid for time away from home and work so it was understandable, but we had him in all the same to question his ambition and just how far he wanted to go. Antiguans have very limited opportunities to play abroad because they aren't in the top seventy in the world and it isn't easy to get a visa on that basis.

There were some amazing athletes and while they were tough kids, most of them lacked the drive, determination and focus to progress further than their comfort zone. For someone as intense as me, I had to buy into them for them to buy into me. I became more flexible in my approach in order to get a viable working relationship because these lads had never had any real discipline in their lives or a set schedule to abide by. When they told me there was no point in getting flustered and to relax, I just had to smile and go with the flow. It was a fabulous place and I couldn't have enjoyed my time there more but it was great to have Paula and the kids come out for the last two weeks because I had really missed them and I didn't want to miss the kids growing up any more than I had to.

The Antiguan FA were delighted with my work and wanted me to stay, but I would have only done that if it had been on a permanent contract, something they could never have committed to. It wasn't how they worked out there. It was short-term planning and not much more and anyway the truth was I didn't want to be away from the family for a longer period. I returned to England feeling revitalised and rested. Willie would return to England himself a few months later and is now at Newcastle United as a development coach. As for me, I picked up exactly where I had left off at Northwich with my Antiguan adventure now no more than a happy memory.

There was plenty to be positive about in terms of our first full season at the club, despite starting on minus ten points for going into administration the previous season. We would be playing our football in the Conference North, having been relegated from the Conference Premier, and we managed to keep our captain, Simon Grand, and also Northwich stalwart Johnny Allen, two key players for the promotion push. We also brought in Mark Danks and Ian

Herring, who we had worked with at Worcester. We started with six or seven players, with the big earners all having left during the summer and began the season trying to wipe out the points deficit as quickly as we could. We made a reasonably good start and within a month, we were back to zero.

We had no real target for the season. It was more a case of putting one foot in front of the other and trying to make as much progress as possible. At Worcester our good FA Cup run brought considerable financial benefits and had set the club up for a whole year. In all honesty, that was Vics' only real hope of being able to turn a pretty dire financial situation around. So the cup took on even greater importance for us in 2009/10.

If we had been knocked out in the preliminary rounds, I am not sure what would have happened to us. We drew Bardon Hill Sports from the East Leicestershire League in our first match. They were unbeaten that season, but they didn't cause us any problems because we thrashed them 8–0, with Mark Danks grabbing five goals and being voted player of the round. He also won two FA Cup final tickets for his performance, which was great.

We pulled Chorley out of the hat next. They were doing well in their league and although they were a better side than Bardon, we scored two early goals and went on to win 4–0. If we could successfully negotiate the next round, we would be in the first-round proper. There was still the chance of a money-spinner, even at that stage of the competition, and we potentially had one, depending on who won the replay between our next opponents, Stalybridge Celtic and FC United of Manchester. Drawing FC was like hitting the jackpot in non-league football because they had such a great following. After holding Stalybridge on their own ground, against the odds, FC won the replay 1–0.

FC United brought a large following with them and the crowd was close to three thousand with their fans probably outnumbering ours. They helped make it a great atmosphere, singing and chanting throughout the game, and they gave me some stick because of my City connections, but it was good-natured banter, nothing more. After a tight ninety minutes, we came out on top, winning by three goals to nil.

That meant we were in round one with the possibility of drawing a genuinely big club, which would guarantee live television coverage. I watched the draw at home with Paula and the kids and because I was Sky-plussing it and pausing for a few seconds as each team came out of the hat, I probably fell a minute or so behind the live draw. Most of the big guns had been pulled out by the time we were given a home tie. Once again I paused the television, wondering whether we would get a big fish or a minnow. Suddenly, I started getting a few texts through, then the house phone went three times and I thought, 'Christ, are Man City or Chelsea still in the hat?' I pressed play and watched as Charlton Athletic's number came out alongside ours, realising instantly that we were one of only three possible games that television would want to cover.

Preecey and I knew from our Worcester days that the spinoffs were incredible, not only the fee from the television company but also the sponsorship and advertising possibilities. We met with Jim Rushe and told him he had to make sure we were one of the chosen games. However, he didn't need to do a thing because ITV had already confirmed that we would be the one of the televised games, with the club receiving £100,000 for the coverage. It was a no-brainer for them, with a non-league side facing a team who were a Premier League outfit just three years before. The sniff of an upset is reason enough for the media and we hoped that we wouldn't disappoint them.

In the run-up to the game, the town was buzzing and I went to watch Charlton at Carlisle a week or so before the tie. Having seen them in the flesh I honestly reckoned we could beat them, an opinion that I passed on to the lads and the chairman. Gradually, people bought into my confident prediction, especially after watching a video of Charlton's previous three games, which proved they had no outstanding individuals in their team and lacked a real presence at set plays. Our game plan was not to engage play until they approached the halfway line, which is ideal if you can keep the score at 0–0 but not such a good idea if you went behind.

In the run-up to the cup tie we majored on set plays, including throw-in routines, something that Dave Kemp had instilled in me as a youngster at Plymouth, where we won many games using his methods.

It is no coincidence that the best set-piece side in the Premier League is Stoke City, where Kempy is assistant manager to Tony Pulis. Fate was working in our favour because after the draw was made our next two games were called off due to inclement weather, so Charlton never got the chance to watch us live.

It meant that when the tie came around we caught them on the hop, causing them all kinds of problems with our set pieces while they scarcely troubled us. Then, on seventy-seven minutes, a young Northwich lad who had signed for us from college, Wayne Riley, came off the bench to score a late winner. It was a fairytale FA Cup story and a wonderful day for the club.

The town celebrated long and hard and even more so when we pulled out Lincoln City at home in round two. It was a great draw and meant we would be facing one of my old teammates, Chris Sutton, who was in charge at Sincil Bank. ITV didn't hesitate in choosing us for live coverage again. It was incredible publicity for the club and for the town and 4,500 people crammed in to see us play even better than we had against Charlton. This time, however, we fell behind first, and although we drew level, we got caught out by two simple balls over the top and lost 3–1. We had caused Lincoln lots of problems but it wasn't our day and our FA Cup adventure was over.

Our next game was a case of after the Lord Mayor's show. On the Tuesday, for a league game, we attracted just 450 fans. Our cup run had counted for nothing as far as bringing in new fans was concerned and it was a massive wake up call. No matter what we did, there would only ever be a hardcore of five hundred fans. Nevertheless, we plodded on and were doing well, getting to within two points of the playoffs despite the ten-point deduction. Then the chairman dropped a bombshell. He called us in to say that our finances weren't stacking up, that the FA still had all our FA Cup money and that in consequence we were going to have to let players go. Matt Bailey, Jon D'Laryea and Simon Grand all went out the door and we had to crack on with the lads we had left. Not surprisingly we didn't make the playoffs after falling away towards the end of the season; in fact we finished twelfth. We had a transfer embargo on us all season and we had also fallen foul of the Conference's dreaded Appendix E, which imposes very strict rules on clubs in administration.

The upshot was that we were relegated again, which meant we had now dropped down two leagues in successive years and would be playing the 2010/11 season in the Evo Stick Northern Premier Division. The club was stumbling from one crisis to another. All our players bar three were released at the end of May and we began the new campaign with just Michael Connor, Michael Aspin and Wayne Riley. Then Aspin decided he didn't want to play for us anymore. It was an almost impossible situation and, unable to attract new players because of the uncertainty about which league we would be playing in, we had to make do with a host of trialists plus Connor and Riley. At our first pre-season, Thursday training session I had two players plus two lads who had turned up on a motorbike from Stoke. Although they both had bellies I didn't have the heart to turn them away so I let them join in, but they crashed out during the warm up! We had been running around the pitch and they had fallen a hundred yards behind. I stopped and waited for them.

'Lads, where exactly have you been playing your football?'

'Oh we haven't played for a bit. We were playing Sunday League in Stoke a couple of years ago and we heard there was a trial at Northwich so we thought we'd give it a go.'

That's where we were, reduced to Sunday League lads chancing their arm. I told them to go and get themselves fit and maybe try again after they could last more than a four-hundred-metre run.

By hook or by crook we gradually built the team back up, through our many contacts in the game. It was hard going but eventually we managed to put quite a decent unit together. We began the season well, punching above our weight, even topping the league briefly. But we were coming off after games wondering how we had not been found out because we were desperately short of quality.

It got so bad at one point that Preecey, my son Arron and I started to play! We took part in the Mid-Cheshire Cup and were playing Middlewich with Arron in goal. We were 1-0 up with a couple of minutes to go and I said to Preecey to get us on so that I could say I'd played in the same game as my lad. He smiled and told me to get ready to come on, which I did. My fatherly pride lasted just thirty seconds, because Middlewich equalised with almost the last kick of the game. Fuck me! Just my luck. There would now be thirty minutes of extra time. Before that, in injury time, a ball went over the top and, as I slid to clear it, Arron raced out towards me and we collided, with his knee connecting with my pelvic bone to the point that I thought he'd broken my hip. Morrison taken out by Morrison. Didn't I say I always made things happen? We had used all our subs so I had to stay on, and I was feeling the pain, but I told Preecey I was okay and we ended up winning 4–1.

Preecey and I both played in the next round against Barnton and he scored a hat-trick in the space of twenty minutes. It put us in the final against Winsford, which we won after extra time and penalties. We also ended the 2010/11 season in mid-table. As for Arron, he's doing all right as a keeper and he gets better every time he plays. He never gives less than his all and he helps the senior keeper out at training so we'll see how he goes. I hope Northwich Vics are on the rise again and if I have played a part in that, I'll be happy for the club and the fans because they deserve a break.

22

It's Not Where You're From...

While Preecey and I battled to make a fist of it at Northwich, apparently I'd been named manager of the Seychelles national team! Just imagine, instead of taking on Retford on a freezing night in Nottinghamshire, I was, allegedly, relaxing on a white sandy beach after training the boys, staring into an aqua blue ocean. Well, if you believe what you read in the papers, that was the scenario. Ex-Manchester City and Blackburn defender Andy Morrison was on Paradise Island at the same time that the other Andy Morrison was turning out against Middlewich. Confused? I was. So were a lot of other people.

It began in September 2010 when I got a phone call from a reporter in Plymouth telling me they had run a big piece in the *Sunday Independent* regarding my appointment as Seychelles coach. I told him he was mistaken and that it was Antigua I had been coaching in, not the Seychelles. Two idyllic island paradises; I just thought they'd got the two places mixed up, but when it was mentioned again by someone else, I had a quick look on Wikipedia and saw it for myself. In my entry, it claimed I was the Seychelles boss. I thought someone would eventually realise the mistake and remove it, but then I started getting a few more calls.

A guy at *World Sport* in Germany wanted to talk to me about how I had got the Seychelles post and I told him there had been a bit of confusion and that it was Antigua I had been to, but he was insistent.

'No, it's right. I've been on the official Seychelles FA website and it says Andy Morrison is the manager. It even has quotes from you about taking the job on.'

I obviously needed to dig into this a bit deeper in case it was a case of identity theft of some sort. I did some research of my own on the Seychelles official website. Sure enough, there was an Andy Morrison, who had apparently played for Manchester City, talking about being the Seychelles manager. He did it quite cleverly and never actually said that he had played either for City or Blackburn, but when people asked if he would be using the contacts he had made in the game, he didn't deny it. The guy claimed that he had a career in England, which had ended early, and that he didn't want to make the same mistakes again. It was something I might have said. It turned out he was indeed called Andy Morrison – Andrew Amers-Morrison to be precise – but that he had never played league football. He had trials, but had not played for anyone of any note. It seemed that wires had been crossed early in the interview process and, after seeing the favourable reaction, he didn't stop it when he perhaps should have done.

In fact, when the story was picked up by the press, the other Andy Morrison was hauled in front of the Seychelles FA to explain the situation. He claimed that he had seen the inference that he was, in fact, me, a couple of days after signing his six-month contract, but despite informing the Seychelles FA of his true identity, officials had failed to remove the incorrect information. Later it was claimed they had had given him the job because they thought he was Andy Morrison of Manchester City fame, so there's hope for me yet! I might one day manage one of those beautiful islands and live the life of Robinson Crusoe. In fact, my application for the Maldives boss vacancy is in the post as we speak! Whatever the truth is, I say fair play to him. At the time of writing, he was going to be allowed to see his six-month probation out so who knows? Maybe he'll be the next Jose Mourinho. We'll have to wait and see what happens. With any luck, he'll do a fucking fantastic job and I'll be able to stick it on my CV!

All of which brings me sort of up to the present. I'm enjoying working at Northwich but I will be looking to branch out on my own at some point. I feel I am almost ready to move into management but I know it won't be as easy. But whatever happens in the future,

I owe a lot to my chairman at Vics, Jim Rushe. After what happened at Worcester, it would have been easy for him to say, 'You're fucking joking, aren't you?' when Preecey suggested me as his number two. I'm not stupid. I know my reputation arrives a long time before I do and that a lot of people wouldn't give me the time of day. Yet Jim gave me a chance to get back into the game and begin a journey that I hope will end in management. He is a real character, a one-off in many ways. He's got a temper worse than mine and we've had our fair share of heated exchanges but only because we both want what is best for the club. He is stubborn, but he has also got bucket loads of enthusiasm and determination, stuff that money can't buy. Being chairman of a non-league club is a thankless task because you can't win whatever you do. What I admire about him is his work ethic – he never stops. Before a game against Buxton everything pointed to the game being called off. There had been heavy snow in Cheshire in the days leading up to the game and on the Friday morning I told him the match was definitely going to be called off.

'No it won't. I'll get it on.'

'You can't beat nature, Jim.'

'Yes I can,' he assured me and I could see he meant it. At eleven that night he was still out on a snowplough trying to clear the pitch so that the game could go ahead. That's the sort of man he is.

The following day I reminded him even he couldn't beat nature.

'It didn't beat me,' he said. 'It wasn't the snow. The pitch was clear but it froze.'

A great character and another reason I love being involved with football. I'll add to that: if you ask David Boddy, the chairman at Worcester, and Jim Rushe and Vics, about my abilities as a coach, both will give me a glowing reference.

My next challenge is finding another club that will show me the faith Jim has in me. I know it won't be easy, but I'm certain it will happen. Sitting down and writing my life story hasn't been easy and I've gone over ground I never thought I would talk openly about. It would have been easy to leave a load of stuff out but, with me, what you see is what you get. Unless it was all or nothing the project wasn't worth undertaking and I'm not glorifying anything, just remembering things exactly the way they happened.

I needed to exorcise one or two ghosts along the way, but it was hard at times. It's all right talking about events and scribbling them down on paper, but when you sit down to read them in one fell swoop, it's an eye-opener. What the writing process has made me realise is that, in many ways, I should never have reached the level I did in the game and played for some of the clubs I did. Not because I wasn't good enough, but because everything in my life was designed to stop me making something of myself. The violence, the drinking and the rage should have stopped me in my tracks, yet I overcame every hurdle. I knocked a few over, but I kept on going and that's down to raw determination and strength of character. Those traits will help me get to the top in coaching.

There's an old saying that I've always liked: 'When the teacher is ready, the pupils will appear.' That's how I see my coaching career progressing. When I'm ready, and the time is right, the opportunity will arise. Whoever takes me on won't regret it. That I'm coaching in the Evo-Stick League is no doubt due to my off-field activities over the years and that's going to stop a lot of chairmen employing me. People ask me when certain jobs crop up, why I've not applied for them. It is because I haven't got a fucking prayer. People get jobs by being in the right place at the right time and that is how it will happen for me.

Do I have a dream job? Well, I'd like to ground myself and build up steadily, but I'd love to be part of taking Plymouth Argyle back to where they belong. I gave my life for them as a fan, I would have fucking died for them as a player and they are my hometown club. I'd love to go back there with the same enthusiasm and drive I had as a kid and help push them back up. They went into administration in March 2011 and were then relegated from League One and are now just one bad season away from the Conference. How the fuck has that happened? Returning to Plymouth some day is top of my list.

Ultimately, I would love to coach in the Premier League and people like Ian Holloway inspire me. He is a special person because he doesn't conform to the identikit of the typical football manager. He is just Ollie. If things don't work out at Blackpool, he'll go somewhere else and do it all over again. He won't become something he's not to protect himself or to save his job. He will do it the Ian Holloway way. He won't say 'yes sir, no sir, three bags full sir' to the chairman so that he can keep his job and appease the fans. With Ian it's all about honesty and doing the right thing. Who wouldn't admire a man like that?

Wherever I end up, I will need everyone to buy into my way of thinking, from the chairman to the players, from the coaching staff to the supporters and from the groundsman to the tea lady. We will play football, but we will want to win, without resorting to the old Wimbledon-type mentality of bludgeoning teams into submission. I will need people who have guts and a strong work ethic. When I was at City, everyone bought into the idea that we were going to get out of the second division, but that we were going to do it together. The thinking was, 'It's shit and it can't get any worse so let's fucking have it.' When you have that kind of chemistry in your club, you can only be successful. It becomes an unstoppable force, an explosion of energy and belief because when you're away to Colchester United on a wet Friday night in November, you can't stand around thinking 'What am I doing here? I'm better than this.' You have to stick your chest out, put on your war paint and say, 'We're fucking having this tonight because we're going to get out of this division' and then you take that mentality out on to the pitch. It's infectious, trust me.

It is going to be hard to get where I want to be. I have got a lot of work to do and I will need to convince people that I am worth a chance, but what you are guaranteed when you take me on is the real deal and somebody who will give everything it takes to be the best.

Regrets? Yeah, I've got plenty, but I can't change the mistakes I've made. All I can do is to learn from them. If standing your ground and not taking any crap is a crime, I'm guilty as charged. There are some things I wish had never happened but there is also plenty I'm proud of. I think I'm a good husband and a great dad – I'm as soft as they come in that respect – and I enjoyed my playing career immensely. I am proud that I captained Argyle and that I ended up skippering Blackpool, Huddersfield Town and once led Manchester City out at Wembley. I am proud that the fans of those clubs were incredible with me and, no matter what happened off the pitch, they backed me. That's because I never let them down on a match day.

If, as people say, I did help City get back to where they belong – by as Joe says, 'dragging the team up, kicking and screaming' – that will be my proudest achievement. I think Andy Morrison and Manchester City were just right for each other at that point in history and I am so grateful that the supporters still treat me like a king whenever I'm in their company. If that's not something to be proud of, I don't know what is.

Life is funny because I had always been waiting to arrive and live happily ever after, like in *Little House on the Prairie*. The truth is, however, is that none of us ever really arrives. Life is a journey, not a destination. Good times come and good times go. The shit times will always be lurking in the background and the good times never seem to last long enough. We will all be tested many times in the days, weeks, months and years ahead, but I've reached a stage where, from here on in, I feel better equipped to deal with whatever life throws at me.

Each day I wake by making a commitment: 'Today, no matter what good or bad occurs in my life, I will not drink.' Then, last thing at night, I say thank you for another day free from alcohol. I have done the same thing since I gave up drinking in February 1999. If I don't strictly follow my routines I am afraid that I will go back to the dark days of alcoholism and out-of-control violence. I don't wallow in the misery of how I behaved when I was drunk, but I always want to be acutely aware of the pain and devastation of what picking up a drink would do to me.

A day will come when I will put my elbows out and there will be wood either side of me. When that happens, I want to lie there, content that I did things my way. I don't want to have regrets and, come or hell high water, success or failure, I'll know I've been true to myself.

One day at a time.

23

Dream Team

Something I've been asked throughout my career, and especially after I stopped playing, was: who would be in your personal all-time team? It is no easy task when you consider some of the guys I've been lucky enough to play alongside, but it's just a bit of fun, so here goes:

Keeper: Nicky Weaver

For two seasons, Nicky was the best young keeper in the country. During the Championship season following our playoff triumph, he won many games for us through a series of brilliant displays. One of those displays, in a 1–0 win over Ipswich, was the best I've ever seen from a goalkeeper. Injuries at important times and, I suggest, a fondness for the bright lights of Manchester prevented Nicky from realising his full potential, but, for me, he was a fantastic keeper who should have got to the very top.

Left back: John Uzzell

The best left back to ever wear the green shirt of Argyle. I used to stand on the Devonport End shouting 'Uuuzzzzzzeeeelllll!' with five thousand others and it was fantastic to hear that echo around Home Park. A great pro and as hard as nails on the pitch, although his missus wore the trousers off the pitch – and she still does!

Right back: Henning Berg

A terrific pro, who I watched develop into one of the best right backs in the game. He took what he was shown on the training pitch into games and was a real gentleman as well.

Centre back: Colin Hendry

A great competitor, strong in the air, he won more challenges and made more blocks in the box than any other defender I played with. Always gave 100 per cent.

Centre back: Richard Dunne

City's best and most consistent performer of the past ten years. He overcame a few personal problems early in his career to become a legend with the fans. Could still have been at the club if Mark Hughes had more belief in him and if his name had been Ricardo Dunninho!

Left wing: Mark Kennedy

The best left-footed player I've ever seen. Could cross a ball on the run and possessed a thunderbolt shot. He made the biggest impact during City's 1999/2000 season and getting him in was an incredible piece of business by Joe Royle.

Right wing: Stuart Ripley

Best crosser of a ball I've ever seen. He had no real tricks, but just moved the ball and crossed with great quality. He never stopped working and made Henning Berg's job a lot easier. If any young player wants to know the responsibilities of being an out-and-out winger, watch a DVD of Ripley in action. He lost a lot of money to me in futile arm-wrestling contests; those north-east boys just don't know when to stop . . .

Centre midfield: David Batty

The most impressive all-round midfielder I played with. If he could have added goals to his game, he would have been one of the best in the country. He could play, he could tackle and, most importantly, he could dictate the pace of play, the mark of true quality. He was never given the credit he deserved.

Centre midfield: Ian Bishop

What a great footballer. He could paint pictures in the middle of the park and never got stuck in possession due to his built-in radar. Whenever he received the ball, he used it well and never gave it away. He was great for centre backs to play with and he would always ask for the ball, marked or unmarked. Bish knows how good he should have been.

Striker: Alan Shearer

All-round striker who led the line superbly. He scored all sorts of goals: headers, tap-ins and beauties from outside the box. Held the ball up brilliantly and was as tough as they come.

Striker: Tommy Tynan

Greatest striker of all time. Enough said!

Substitutes:

Eyal Berkovic:

A genius on the football pitch.

Chris Sutton:

Scored and made goals and a great lad to boot.

Shaun Goater

Purely because of the goals he scored and the impact he had during the 1999/2000 season. Scored for fun and wasn't fussy which part of his body he put them in with. Got so many vital goals for us and won us a load of points in games that were nip and tuck.

Tim Flowers

A fantastic keeper, who helped win the title for Blackburn the season before I arrived, in much the same way that Nicky Weaver did during the 1999/2000 season for City.

Nick Marker:

A good friend of mine who I watched as a youngster and later played alongside. Fit, could play, strong in the tackle, a willing runner and was never intimidated by anyone.

Manager: Joe Royle

It would have to be Joe. He wanted you to become a good player but it meant just as much to him if you became a good man. You never felt like a piece of meat with Joe. He wanted you to look after your family first and serve the club well second.

Coach: Willie Donachie

For the same reasons as Joe. He was another guy who cared about a player's welfare as much as he did about his ability on the pitch. In addition, Willie has had such a positive effect on my life and has helped me to progress so much as a coach.

ANDY MORRISON CAREER STATISTICS

Plymouth Argyle:

1987/88	Played 1	Scored 0 goals	(Division 2)
1988/89	Played 2	Scored 0 goals	(Division 2)
1989/90	Played 19	Scored 1 goal	(Division 2)
1990/91	Played 32	Scored 2 goals	(Division 2)
1991/92	Played 30	Scored 3 goals	(Division 2)
1992/93	Played 29	Scored 0 goals	(Division 2)

Transferred on 5 August 1993 for £500,000

Blackburn Rovers:

1993/94	Played 5	Scored 0 goals	(Premiership)
1994/95	Played 0	Scored 0 goals	(Premiership)

Transferred on 9 December 1994 for £245,000

Blackpool:

1994/95	Played 18	Scored 0 goals	(Division 2)
1995/96	Played 29	Scored 3 goals	(Division 2)

Transferred on 4 July 1996 for £500,000

Huddersfield Town:

1996/97	Played 10	Scored 1 goal	(Division 1)
1997/98	Played 23	Scored 1 goal	(Division 1)
1998/99	Played 12	Scored 0 goals	(Division 1)

Transferred on 29 October 1998 for £80,000

Manchester City:

1998/99	Played 22	Scored 4 goals	(Division 2)
1999/00	Played 12	Scored 0 goals	(Division 1)
2000/01	Played 3	Scored 0 goals	(Premiership)

Blackpool*

2000/01	Played 6	Scored 1 goal	(Division 3)

Crystal Palace*

2000/01	Played 5	Scored 0 goals	(Division 1)

Sheffield United*

2000/01	Played 4	Scored 0 goals	(Division 1)

Manchester City:

2001/02	Played 0	Scored 0 goals	(Division 1)

* On loan